The

FABULOUS

DINOSAUR

FACTFILE

p

This is a Parragon Book
First published in 2000

Parragon
Queen Street House
4 Queen Street
Bath BA1 1HE, UK

Produced by
Monkey Puzzle Media Ltd
Gissing's Farm
Fressingfield
Suffolk IP21 5SH
UK

ISBN 0-75254-437-3

Printed in Spain

AUTHORS
Paul Dowswell, John Malam,
Paul Mason, Steve Parker

ILLUSTRATORS
John Butler, Chris Christoforou, John Egan, Roger Goode,
Philip Hood (Wildlife Art), Mark Iley (Wildlife Art), David McAllister,
Martin McKenna (Sarah Brown Agency), Michael Posen,
Steve D White and Brian Williamson, Tim White

DESIGNERS
Tessa Barwick, Sarah Crouch, Tim Mayer, Victoria Webb

EDITOR
Katie Orchard

ARTWORK COMMISSIONING
Roger Goddard-Coote

PROJECT MANAGER
Alex Edmonds

ADDITIONAL EDITORIAL ASSISTANCE FROM
Michael Flaherty, Caroline Hamilton and Lynda Lines

Contents

What is a Dinosaur?

THE YEAR OF THE DINOSAUR

Every story has a beginning, and for the magnificent creatures we call dinosaurs their story begins in 1841. In that year, the British Association for the Advancement of Science held its annual meeting at Plymouth, a town on the south coast of England. One of the speakers was Professor Richard Owen, a scientist and animal expert, who was also a friend of Queen Victoria.

For several years Owen had been studying animal fossils, particularly the huge bones of ancient reptiles. Most scientists believed these bones were the remains of prehistoric crocodiles and gigantic lizards, but Owen thought that this was wrong. The more he looked at the old bones, the more certain he was that they came from a new group of animals – a group which was completely unknown to science.

At the meeting in Plymouth, Owen spoke for more than two hours to the leading scientists of his day. What astonished them was the fact that

CHINESE DRAGONS

The Chinese were the first people to write about dinosaurs, although they didn't know it at the time. About 1700 years ago, Chang Qu, a Chinese writer, described how "dragon bones" had been found in Wucheng, a region in the middle of the country. Today's scientists think that they were dinosaur bones, and the area that they came from is one of the best places in China to search for their ancient remains.

Owen wasn't talking about the discovery of just one new animal. Instead, he was talking about a completely new group which might contain tens, hundreds, or even thousands of different animals. It was one of the greatest discoveries of the 1800s, and it changed the way that people thought about life on Earth.

Tyrannosaurus rex was probably one of the most fearsome of the "terrible lizards" and the best-known of the dinosaurs.

Richard Owen

In 1854, Richard Owen helped to open a dinosaur park in Crystal Palace, London. The park contained life-sized models of dinosaurs.

DINOSAUR CHARACTERISTICS

Today's scientists use the following basic rules to decide whether the ancient creatures they are looking at are dinosaurs:
- dinosaurs lived between 250–65 million years ago;
- they lived on land;
- they could not fly;
- they had straight legs tucked underneath their bodies;
- they were reptiles.

FINDING A NAME

Owen's group of animals needed a name. At his talk in 1841, Owen had not used a name, but when he wrote about his ideas in 1842 he used the name "Dinosauria". He made the name from two Greek words: *deinos*, meaning "terrible" and *sauros*, meaning "lizard". From then on there was a new word in the English language – dinosaur.

WERE ALL PREHISTORIC CREATURES DINOSAURS?

Although many other animals lived at the same time as the dinosaurs, they belonged to different groups. Some could fly and some lived in the seas and oceans, so these prehistoric creatures were not dinosaurs. However, their story is just as interesting and important as that of the dinosaurs, since they, too, have played their part in the development of life on Earth.

When Did Dinosaurs Live?

WHEN EARTH BELONGED TO THE DINOSAURS
The animal kingdom is a huge collection of species – one estimate suggests there are as many as 10–15 million different kinds of creatures alive on the Earth today. Animals come in all shapes and sizes, and live in all environments, and it was just like this when dinosaurs lived on Earth, too.

A popular name for the time when dinosaurs lived is the "Age of Dinosaurs". This was a long time which lasted for about 185 million years. Humans, on the other hand, have lived on Earth for only about 2 million years. It's very difficult to imagine such great spans of time, since we are more used to thinking about time in terms of days, months, and years. A simple explanation is that planet Earth belonged to the dinosaurs for about ninety times longer than it has belonged to humans.

THE AGE OF DINOSAURS
Earth is an old planet. Scientists think that it formed about 4,500 million years ago. They divide the whole of Earth's long existence into intervals of time, each of which represents a chapter in the story of the planet.

About 600 million years ago, a new chapter began. Scientists call this the Phanerozoic Eon. It is divided into three smaller parts called eras. The oldest part is the Paleozoic Era, which was followed by the Mesozoic Era, which in turn was followed by the Cenozoic Era.

The Mesozoic Era is the scientific name for the Age of Dinosaurs. It was during the Mesozoic that dinosaurs appeared, and then died out. Humans appeared during the Cenozoic Era, an interval of time which continues right up to the present day. The following table shows how the three eras fit together.

Pre-Cambrian

Cambrian

Ordovician

Silurian

Devonian

Era	Meaning	Millions of years ago	Which animals appeared?
Cenozoic	"recent life"	65 to the present day	mammals, including humans
Mesozoic	"middle life"	250 –65	dinosaurs
Palaeozoic	"ancient life"	600 –250	fishes, amphibians, reptiles

THE MESOZOIC ERA

The Mesozoic Era is divided into three periods – the Triassic, Jurassic, and Cretaceous. You can see how these periods fit together in the following table:

Period	Millions of years ago	What happened to dinosaurs?
Cretaceous	144 – 65	the last dinosaurs
Jurassic	206–144	the greatest time for dinosaurs
Triassic	250 –206	the first dinosaurs

Jurassic

Triassic

Permian

Tertiary

Carboniferous

Quaternary

THE MEANING OF "JURASSIC"

The Jurassic Period is named after the Jura Mountains, which lie in eastern France. These mountains are made from limestone, a rock that occurs in many parts of the world. Plant and animal fossils, including dinosaur remains, are found in limestone which formed during the Jurassic Period.

The Earth's Changing Shape

**The world in the Triassic Period
250–206 million years ago**

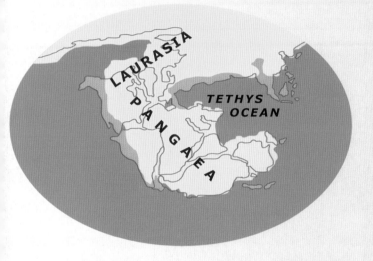

In the Triassic, Earth's land was joined together in one huge supercontinent known as Pangaea. The animals that lived on Pangaea, including the first dinosaurs, were free to wander in all directions since there were no oceans to stop them from crossing the continent.

**The world in the Jurassic Period
206–144 million years ago**

During the Jurassic, Pangaea was split apart by huge cracks that opened up in the Earth's crust. The process of continental drift had begun, pulling North America, Europe and Asia away from South America, Africa and Australia. Oceans flooded the gaps between the continents, creating watery barriers which land animals – including dinosaurs – could no longer cross.

A RESTLESS PLANET

Throughout its long history, Earth has been shaped by the forces of nature. It is these powerful forces which gave the land and oceans their shape, and which continue to change the planet even today. The action of some forces, such as volcanoes and glaciers, is easy to see. But the action of other forces is far less obvious.

THE GIANT JIGSAW PUZZLE

When we look at a map of the world, it is as if we are looking at the pieces of a giant jigsaw puzzle. It seems that if we could move the continents around some of them would fit together. For example, the bulge of South America seems to fit into the hollow of Africa – the only problem is that they are separated by the Atlantic Ocean.

For hundreds of years, scholars had been puzzled by the shape of the continents. As early as 1596, Abraham Ortelius suggested that America had been torn away from Europe and Africa by earthquakes and floods – but his ideas were not taken seriously. It wasn't until 1915 that a German scientist, Alfred Wegener, came up with a solution to the mystery.

SLOWLY BUT SURELY

Continents move incredibly slowly, at a rate of as little as 1-4 centimetres (⅜–1½ inches) a year. Over the course of millions of years, these tiny measurements add up to account for the drift of the continents across the Earth.

These maps show how the shapes of the Earth's land masses have changed during the last 250 million years. The land is coloured yellow, and the sea blue. The areas that make up today's continents are shown outlined in dark blue.

The world in the Cretaceous Period 144–65 million years ago

By the time of the Cretaceous the continents had more or less reached their present-day positions. Each continent was stocked with its own variety of unique animals.

The world as it is today

The world today is divided into seven continents – but as the process of continental drift is never-ending, these land masses continue to move little by little each year. In the future, the map of the world will look different again.

Wegener said that the Earth's continents had started off as one huge mass of land – a supercontinent which he called Pangaea, meaning "All Earth". He said that during the Mesozoic Era, forces from deep inside the Earth began to crack Pangaea into smaller pieces. Then, over millions of years, the pieces drifted across the face of the Earth until they reached the stage they are at today.

A POWERFUL FORCE

For many years no one knew what force was strong enough to move continents. The answer was found in the early 1960s, when scientists discovered that the Earth's top layer, or crust, was cracked into giant pieces of land, which they called plates. On top of these plates were the continents.

In the oceans, magma, which is molten rock from deep inside the planet, is constantly forced up to the surface. The magma makes new crust, and pushes outward the older crust already formed. It is this force coming from within the Earth itself that moves the plates, which carry the continents with them. This process is called continental drift.

The World of the Dinosaurs

TRIASSIC PERIOD (250–206 MILLION YEARS AGO)

LAND   All land was joined together in the supercontinent called Pangaea.

CLIMATE   The temperature on land was constantly dry and warm.

PLANTS   Trees such as conifers and ginkgoes flourished, as did tree ferns, horse-tails and cycads. There were no flowering plants.

DINOSAURS   The first dinosaurs appeared – small two-legged meat eaters, and larger plant eaters that walked on two or four legs.

OTHER ANIMALS   Insects, crocodiles, small mammals, frogs, turtles, fish, gliding lizards and flying pterosaurs.

Triassic landscape

JURASSIC PERIOD (206–144 MILLION YEARS AGO)

LAND   Pangaea began to crack apart, forming smaller land masses separated by sea.

CLIMATE   The temperature became cooler and rainfall increased.

PLANTS   Conifer forests covered vast areas of land, and ginkgoes, palms, tree ferns and horse-tails flourished in the moist climate. There were still no flowering plants.

DINOSAURS   Giant-sized plant-eating dinosaurs appeared which fed on the lush vegetation. Large meat eaters lived at this time, too.

OTHER ANIMALS   The first birds appeared, but pterosaurs ruled the skies. The ancestors of present-day bees and flies buzzed through the air, while icthyosaurs, plesiosaurs, fish and molluscs lived in the sea.

Jurassic landscape

KEEP OFF THE FERNS!
Grass did not exist during the Age of Dinosaurs. To dinosaurs, the equivalent of grass was ferns.

CRETACEOUS PERIOD (144–65 MILLION YEARS AGO)

LAND   The continents reached their present-day positions, and mountain ranges were formed where plates pushed into each other.

CLIMATE   The temperature continued to cool down. There were wet and dry seasons, which gradually changed into summer and winter seasons.

PLANTS   The first flowering plants appeared. They spread quickly and became the main type of ground-covering plants. Oak, maple, walnut and beech trees grew alongside the still abundant conifers, cycads and ferns.

DINOSAURS   Herds of small plant-eating dinosaurs roamed across open countryside, preyed upon by meat-eating predators. Some dinosaurs developed body armour to protect themselves from attack.

Cretaceous landscape

OTHER ANIMALS   Snakes and small mammals appeared on the land, crocodiles lived in freshwater pools, and huge reptiles flew through the skies, as did many kinds of birds and the first moths. Giant turtles and lizard-like animals swam in the seas, feeding on the plentiful supplies of fish and molluscs.

Life Begins

THE FIRST SIGNS OF LIFE

Scientists believe that the Earth was formed 4,500 million years ago and that for the first 1,000 million years of its existence there was no life here. It was a lifeless planet, just like thousands of others in the universe. But then, about 3,500 million years ago, the first signs of life appeared.

LIFE WITHOUT OXYGEN

The air that we breathe today contains oxygen, a gas which living things need in order to stay alive. But the further back you look in time, the less oxygen there was in the atmosphere. In the beginning there was no oxygen at all.

When Earth was a young planet, its atmosphere was made from a mixture of gases, such as carbon dioxide, methane and hydrogen sulphide – the gas that makes rotten eggs smell so bad. These gasses coloured the sky pink, not blue. To oxygen-breathing dinosaurs – and to humans, too – this is a recipe for death, not life. But it was in these hostile conditions that life on Earth began.

Many scientists believe that life on Earth first began in conditions like these, about 3,500 million years ago.

THE "SPARK" OF LIFE

The question "How did life begin?" is one of the biggest questions of all, and it is one which has no easy answer. A simple explanation is that life began as the result of a chemical reaction. It began in Earth's oceans, where energy from lightning, the Sun or even from meteorites that came crashing down, provided the all-important "spark". As the energy was released it set off a chain reaction amongst chemicals in the oceans. As the chemicals reacted with each other, structures called organic molecules were made. Amongst the new molecules were amino acids – the building blocks of life, from which all living things stem. The story of life on Earth had begun.

ALGAE, THE OXYGEN MAKERS

The first living things on Earth were simple, tiny organisms called bacteria. They lived in the oceans, which were not blue as they are today, but rusty red. There were algae too, organisms which lived in shallow water and which spread out across the sea floor in vast colonies, like huge, sticky blankets. These microscopic specks of algae changed the Earth's atmosphere. In their daily lives they made a waste product which they pumped into the oceans. The waste product was oxygen gas.

At first, the oxygen was dissolved into the oceans. Oxygen changed the water's colour from red to blue. Then, after the oceans were filled with oxygen, the time had come for the atmosphere to change, too. Oxygen bubbled up from the algae in the oceans and escaped into the sky. As oxygen filled the atmosphere it took over from carbon dioxide, methane, and hydrogen sulphide. With an atmosphere containing oxygen, the sky's colour changed from pink to blue. This oxygen-rich air could be breathed in – it was time for new forms of life to appear.

LIFE IN A TEST-TUBE

In 1953, the scientist, Stanley Miller, carried out an experiment in a laboratory at the University of Chicago, USA. He created an atmosphere similar to the one which existed on Earth 3,000 million years ago. It was a mixture of the gasses methane, hydrogen and ammonia, to which he added water. Into this "chemical soup" he passed electrical charges which released energy. After a few days Miller found that amino acids had formed – he had the ingredients for life.

Before the Dinosaurs

TIMELINE OF EARLY LIFE ON EARTH

There was life on Earth for about 3,250 million years before the first dinosaurs appeared. The story of early life can be broken down into stages, each one marking a crucial step along the path towards the emergence of the first dinosaurs, some 250 million years ago. This chapter traces the evolution of early life, to the point at which dinosaurs came on to the scene.

PRE-CAMBRIAN PERIOD
3,500–570 MILLION YEARS AGO

For the first 3,000 million years of life on Earth, all life was microscopic – it would have been too small to see with the naked eye. Today, you can only see the remains of these tiny ancient creatures, preserved as microfossils, with the help of a microscope. All life was in the oceans – there was no life on land.

CAMBRIAN PERIOD
570–510 MILLION YEARS AGO

The first creatures big enough to be seen with the naked eye appeared. These were creatures without backbones, the invertebrates, such as molluscs, sponges, worms, jellyfish and starfish. All life was in the oceans.

ORDOVICIAN PERIOD
510–440 MILLION YEARS AGO

Creatures with backbones, the vertebrates, appeared. The oceans were home to corals, trilobites, sponges, jellyfish and graptolites which lived in colonies and floated through the water. All life was in the oceans.

SILURIAN PERIOD
440–410 MILLION YEARS AGO

The first fish with jaws evolved. Coral reefs flourished in the oceans. The first plants grew on land. Scorpions and millipedes came out of the water and adapted to living on land.

THE FIRST MASS EXTINCTION

The first great mass extinction of animals happened at the end of the Permian Period, 250 million years ago, when about three-quarters of all amphibian and reptile species died out on land and half of all species in the oceans. This event is the most catastrophic loss of life ever known on Earth – greater even than the extinction of the dinosaurs. The reasons why so many animal species disappeared at this time are unclear, although most scientists think that it was because of massive changes that happened on a global scale, such as alterations in the climate and the drying up of the oceans.

DEVONIAN PERIOD
410–360 MILLION YEARS AGO

This was the "Age of Fish". Fish dominated life in the seas. The first insects appeared. The first amphibians evolved – creatures that can live in water and on land. Primitive plants formed the first forest on land. Horse-tails and club mosses appeared.

CARBONIFEROUS PERIOD
360–290 MILLION YEARS AGO

Snails, centipedes, millipedes, cockroaches and giant dragonflies thrived in the warm, damp climate. The first small insect-eating reptiles, which evolved from amphibians, appeared. Giant tree ferns, horse-tails and conifers formed forests.

PERMIAN PERIOD
290–250 MILLION YEARS AGO

New species of larger reptiles evolved and took over from amphibians. Ferns, horse-tails and conifers were widespread on the land.

The First Reptiles

WHAT IS A REPTILE?

A reptile is an animal that has all of the following characteristics:

- it must have a backbone;
- it must be cold-blooded;
- it must lay eggs;
- it must have scaly skin.

Turtles, crocodiles, lizards and snakes are examples of living reptiles, but there are many examples of reptiles, such as the dinosaurs, which have died out.

The 1-metre- (3-foot-) long amphibian *Gerrothorax* led a double life, able to crawl on land and swim under water using its webbed feet.

Hylonomus

Hylonomus was an anapsid reptile. It lived 310 million years ago and was one of the first reptiles. Only about 20 centimetres (8 inches) long, its remains have been discovered in Canada, inside the stumps of hollow trees where it may have crawled in search of insects to eat.

FROM AMPHIBIANS TO REPTILES

Towards the end of the Carboniferous Period, about 290 million years ago, the very first reptiles appeared. They evolved from amphibians, which were animals that could live in both water and on land. The very name – amphibian – means "double life". Amphibians were the first animals with backbones to develop legs with feet instead of fins. Having feet meant that amphibians were able to move on the ground. Although amphibians were able to survive on land, they still needed to spend some of their time in water. Unlike amphibians, reptiles lived entirely on dry land. This important difference meant that reptiles did not have to live close to water. Instead, they could wander wherever they liked on land.

Hyperodapedon

Hyperodapedon was a diapsid reptile from 250 million years ago. About 1.3 metres (4 feet) long, it lived on a diet of vegetation which it tore up with its powerful beak. Its remains have been found in Scotland.

Kannameyeria was a synapsid reptile which lived 250 million years ago. It was about 3 metres (10 feet) long and fed on plants which it bit through with its beak and two large dog-like teeth. Its remains have been found in South Africa.

Kannameyeria

Anapsid skull

Synapsid skull

Diapsid skull

REPTILES BEFORE THE DINOSAURS

Towards the end of the Triassic Period, about 230 million years ago, several major groups, or families, of reptiles had evolved. Scientists sort these families into groups based on the appearance of their skulls. Some animals had holes in their skulls which allowed their jaw muscles to contract, or tighten, while others had skulls without holes. There are three main groups of early reptiles, based on the number of openings in their skulls:

• anapsids – reptiles of the "no hole" group had skulls with no muscle holes in them;

• synapsids – reptiles of the "one hole" group had skulls with one muscle hole on either side;

• diapsids – reptiles of the "two hole" group had skulls with two muscle holes on either side.

Dinosaurs and other prehistoric creatures, such as pterosaurs in the sky and ichthyosaurs and plesiosaurs in the oceans, evolved from this group of reptiles. Present-day diapsids include crocodiles, lizards, snakes and birds.

IS LIZZIE THE FIRST REPTILE?

Scientists are not certain which animal counts as the world's first reptile. In 1988, a creature was found in Scotland in rocks that are 350 million years old. Some scientists believe it is the first reptile, but others think it is an amphibian. They have named it *Westlothiana lizziae* after the region of Scotland where it was found. Its nickname is Lizzie.

The First Dinosaurs

THE AGE OF DINOSAURS BEGINS

The first dinosaurs appeared about 228 million years ago. Their ancestors were reptiles that belonged to the diapsid group of animals. For 185 million years dinosaurs were the dominant, or ruling, animals on Earth. But it is important to remember that in all this time dinosaurs were not alone on the planet, since there were many other animals with backbones that lived alongside them. Some of these other prehistoric creatures lived on land too, but others were able to fly and swim. The whole incredible range of these ancient animals formed a worldwide ecosystem in which every creature had its place and in which dinosaurs were the leading animals on land.

Erythrosuchus was an archosaur, an ancestor of the dinosaurs. This meat eater measured up to 5 metres (16 feet) long.

Erythrosuchus

HOW DINOSAURS EVOLVED

In order to know where dinosaurs came from we have to look closely at their diapsid ancestors. Among the diapsids were a number of animals that scientists have called archosaurs, which means "ruling reptiles". These animals were beginning to dominate life on the land. The dinosaur family tree begins with the earliest of the archosaurs – a group of large crocodile-like animals with sprawling legs. Known as thecodonts, which means "socket toothed", they were big, heavy reptiles that crawled on all four legs. Thecodonts were meat-eating animals with long jaws and long tails.

Not all reptiles changed from the sprawling gait to the semi-erect and erect gaits. Some, like the crocodiles, are still "sprawlers" today.

1. Sprawling gait

2. Semi-erect gait

Eoraptor

THE OLDEST KNOWN DINOSAUR

The first dinosaurs were small, lightweight animals. They walked on two legs, ate meat and plants and were probably very agile and fast movers. The earliest known dinosaur is *Eoraptor lunensis*. It lived 228 million years ago. *Eoraptor* was a small, primitive meat eater about 1 metre (3 feet) long. It was discovered in what is now Argentina, South America, in 1991. It was named *Eoraptor*, meaning "dawn raptor", in 1993. Its name tells us that scientists believe it lived at the very beginning of the Age of Dinosaurs.

Eoraptor **walked on two legs and may have been a fast runner. It had light, hollow bones, a long head with many small, sharp teeth and five fingers on its hands.**

FROM CRAWLING TO WALKING

With the emergence of thecodonts, a major stage in the evolution of dinosaurs was complete. But there was still a long way to go before the first true dinosaurs appeared. Early thecodonts walked like modern crocodiles do, with their knees and elbows at right angles to their bodies. They held their bodies close to the ground. Over millions of years, thecodonts evolved and the positions of their limbs changed. Later thecodonts walked in a more upright position and they were able to run, but they still moved on all fours. Smaller, lightly-built thecodonts were the first animals to run for short distances on their back legs. For some animals walking on two legs became the normal means of movement. True dinosaurs came from these creatures.

3. Pillar-erect gait

4. "Typical" erect gait

How Dinosaurs are Classified

THE TWO DINOSAUR ORDERS
In 1887, British geologist, Harry Seeley, came up with a way of dividing dinosaurs into two basic groups, or orders. Over many years he had made a careful study of dinosaur skeletons in museum collections, noting their similarities and differences. He noticed that dinosaur hip bones were either shaped like those of lizards or birds. This important observation led him to propose a new idea – that dinosaurs should be divided into the order *Saurischia* ("lizard-hipped" dinosaurs) and the order *Ornithischia* ("bird-hipped" dinosaurs).

SAURISCHIA – THE "LIZARD-HIPPED" DINOSAURS

Dinosaurs whose hip bones were shaped like those of lizards fall into two types: the agile, meat-eating theropods and the slower-moving, plant-eating sauropods.

THEROPODS
Name means "Beast foot"
Description Dinosaurs which walked on three-toed bird-like feet with sharp claws. They had powerful legs, small arms, a short compact chest, a long muscular tail, a curved and flexible neck, large eyes and long jaws with dagger-like teeth.
Examples *Allosaurus, Baryonyx, Deinonychus, Oviraptor* and *Tyrannosaurus*.
Diet They were carnivores – meat-eating dinosaurs.

SAUROPODS
Name means "Lizard foot"
Description Large- to massive-sized dinosaurs which walked on all four feet. They had small heads, long necks, bulky bodies and long tails.
Examples *Apatosaurus, Brachiosaurus, Diplodocus* and *Seismosaurus*.
Diet They were herbivores – plant-eating dinosaurs.

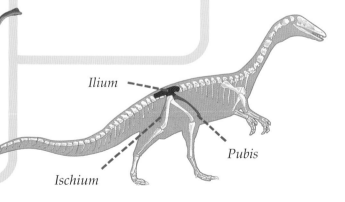

Ilium

Pubis

Ischium

In the skeletons of saurischians the pubis bone of the hip points downwards and to the front.

DINOSAURS

All dinosaurs were descended from reptiles called thecodonts, which first appeared on Earth during the Triassic period.

ORNITHISCHIA – THE "BIRD-HIPPED" DINOSAURS

Dinosaurs whose hip bones were shaped like those of living birds were far more varied than the "lizard-hipped" dinosaurs. These dinosaurs are divided into five types: ankylosaurs, ceratopsians, ornithopods, pachycephalosaurs and stegosaurs.

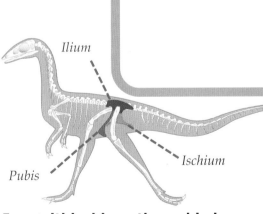

Ilium

Ischium

Pubis

In ornithischians the pubis bone points downwards and towards the tail. The pelvis is wider than that of saurischians. This may have made ornithischians more stable while moving.

ANKYLOSAURS

Name means "Fused-together reptiles"
Description Small to medium-sized dinosaurs. They had low, squat bodies with massive limbs. Their bodies were covered in flexible, bony armour of slabs, plates and spikes, and they had small teeth and weak jaws.
Examples *Ankylosaurus* and *Euoplocephalus*.
Diet They were herbivores – plant eaters.

CERATOPSIANS

Name means "Horned faces"
Description Small to large dinosaurs that moved about on two or four legs. Some had horned and frilled heads and some had narrow parrot-like beaks. They probably lived in large herds.
Examples *Psittacosaurus* and *Triceratops*.
Diet They were herbivores – plant eaters.

ORNITHOPODS

Name means "Bird feet"
Description Small to very large dinosaurs that walked and ran on their two back feet. Some lived in large herds. Some had crests on their heads.
Examples *Lesothosaurus*, *Iguanodon* and *Parasaurolophus*.
Diet They were herbivores – plant eaters.

PACHYCEPHALOSAURS

Name means "Bone heads"
Description Small- to medium-sized dinosaurs. They were slow-moving, had thick skulls and moved about on two back legs. They lived in herds.
Examples *Pachycephalosaurus* and *Stegoceras*.
Diet They were herbivores – plant eaters.

STEGOSAURS

Name means "Roofed reptiles"
Description Medium-sized dinosaurs. They moved about on all-fours and were slow-moving. Their skins were covered in bony plates or spikes, and they had short, weak teeth.
Examples *Kentrosaurus* and *Stegosaurus*.
Diet They were herbivores – plant eaters.

Meat-eating Dinosaurs

SNAPPERS AND CHOMPERS

Most animals today are meat or plant eaters. Just as lions and leopards hunt grazing wildebeest and gazelle, dinosaurs such as *Tyrannosaurus* and *Allosaurus* hunted *Triceratops* or *Iguanodon*.

Hunters need special skills and features to survive – after all, if they do not catch their food, they do not eat. Meat eaters today usually have big teeth, savage claws, sharp eyes and fast legs. Most meat-eating dinosaurs had all these features and more. But not all of them were big-jawed monsters on the look-out for an equally vast walking supper. Some were tiny, vicious pack hunters, barely bigger than a chicken, and some just ate insects, lizards and eggs.

A herd of *Coelophysis* chasing prey. Living in a group gave the smallish dinosaurs some protection from larger predators.

AN EARLY MEAT EATER

Speed was important to many meat-eating dinosaurs. *Coelophysis*, one of the earliest dinosaurs, is a good example of this. It stalked the dry desert-like lands of what is now New Mexico, USA, during the Late Triassic Period. Its upright posture, hollow bones, light build and powerful legs made it a very fast runner.

Although *Coelophysis* was not a large dinosaur, its long neck gave it a good view of approaching prey and predators. It hunted small reptiles and even ate other young *Coelophysis* when there was no other food around.

Like many meat eaters, *Coelophysis* hunted in packs. This allowed it to kill prey far bigger than itself.

Tyrannosaurus rex

WATCH YOUR STEP!

Tyrannosaurus rex was so heavy and tall, it would probably have smashed its skull if it tripped over whilst chasing prey. Its tiny arms were too small to protect it from a fall.

SHARP TEETH AND TALONS

Many dinosaurs relied on special features, such as teeth or claws. *Compsognathus* may have been the smallest meat-eating dinosaur. It roamed the sprawling forests of Germany and France, during the Late Jurassic Period. Including its tail, it was about 0.7 metres (2 feet) long and weighed little more than a chicken. But, despite its size, *Compsognathus* was a deadly predator. It hunted other small animals, such as lizards and insects, which it caught with its small, sharp teeth and grasping talons. With its light build and long legs it shared many of the same features as the earlier dinosaur, *Coelophysis*.

A POWERFUL GIANT

Tyrannosaurus rex was one of the largest meat eaters that ever lived. It lurked in the forests of North America and Asia, waiting to ambush the hefty plant eaters that shared its habitat. At 7 tonnes (7 tons), it weighed more than an African elephant. Its size made it safe from any other dinosaur on the planet, although *Tyrannosaurus* did occasionally fight each other. But its size and build made it a lumbering, clumsy beast. It would certainly have been a lot less agile than other meat eaters. However, *Tyrannosaurus* had a secret weapon – what it lacked in speed, it more than made up for with its powerful jaw. Its mouth was packed with 60 serrated-edge teeth, which could snap off 230 kilograms (500 pounds) of meat in one bite. Its sight and sense of smell were especially good, too. Because it was not a fast runner, it probably lay in wait for its prey, darting out of the forest to kill unsuspecting plant eaters with a single, massive bite.

When *Tyrannosaurus* bit into flesh, it probably pulled back each side of its jaw, in turn, to slice through the meat with its sharp teeth.

Like *Tyrannosaurus*, *Carcharodontosaurus* was a fierce meat eater with massive jaws and very sharp teeth.

Carcharodontosaurus

DEADLY WEAPONS

The *Velociraptor* was one of the most fearsome predators of the Cretaceous Period. Able to run at 60 kph (40 mph), in short bursts, it terrified slow-moving plant eaters on the baking plains of what is now Mongolia and China. Armed with slashing talons on all four limbs, and around 30 very sharp, curved teeth, *Velociraptor* also had a single, retractable, long claw on the middle toe of each foot. It used the claw like a dagger to stab its prey. Although it was relatively small, it hunted in a pack, so it could attack animals much bigger than itself.

One extraordinary fossil find, unearthed in Mongolia in 1971, gives us a clue to the last violent moments of a *Velociraptor's* life. It shows the predator in a duel to the death with a lumbering *Protoceratops*. The *Velociraptor* is grasping the *Protoceratops'* head shield, while slashing at its belly. The *Protoceratops* has pierced the chest of the *Velociraptor* with its horny, beak-like mouth. Both animals died in the battle and crashed to the ground, to be preserved forever in their final death-throes.

THE DINOSAUR WITH A SAIL ON ITS BACK

Some dinosaurs, such as the *Spinosaurus*, had very unusual features. *Spinosaurus* hunted other dinosaurs around Northern Africa, during the Late Jurassic Period. Almost as big as *Tyrannosaurus rex*, it measured 12 metres (39 feet) from nose to tail. Its most impressive feature is the big sail on its back. This may have helped the *Spinosaurus* to control its body temperature. It may also have been used to attract female dinosaurs, or frighten male rivals away. Whatever its use, it seems an awkward attachment for a hunter – making it clumsy and vulnerable to attack.

Spinosaurus was different from most meat eaters in other ways, too. Its teeth were straight, rather than curved and serrated. It also had unusually long arms, so it may have occasionally walked on all fours.

As well as hunting for food, *Spinosaurus*, like many other large meat eaters, was probably a scavenger. It was fierce enough to frighten off all but the largest predators from their own kills.

Spinosaurus probably used its claws and crocodile-like jaws to snap up fishes from lakes and rivers.

Spinosaurus

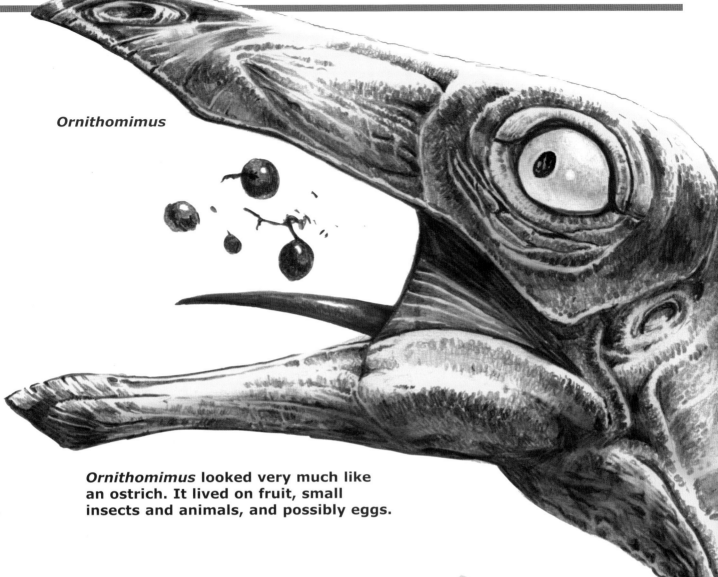

Ornithomimus

Ornithomimus looked very much like an ostrich. It lived on fruit, small insects and animals, and possibly eggs.

A DINOSAUR WITH A BEAK
Some dinosaurs, such as *Ornithomimus*, were omnivores – they ate plant food as well as meat. *Ornithomimus* was about the same size as an ostrich. It lived during the Late Cretaceous Period, in North America and Asia. *Ornithomimus* had a horny beak rather than teeth. It used its clawed fingers to grasp and kill smaller animals such as lizards and mammals. *Ornithomimus* may have been an egg-eating nest-raider, too. If it was disturbed by an angry parent, it could sprint away at 50 kph (30 mph). Fossil remains show that the *Ornithomimus* had a large brain. It is thought by dinosaur experts to be one of the most intelligent dinosaurs.

The skull of the meat eater Allosaurus

BIG BRAINS

Meat eaters had bigger brains than plant eaters. Finding, chasing and catching prey required considerably more thought than wandering around in a herd, munching plants.

27

Plant-eating Dinosaurs

Plateosaurus

Plateosaurus rears up to reach leaves in the trees. It may have used its arms to pull down branches too.

GRAZERS AND GRINDERS

Probably two-thirds of all dinosaurs were plant eaters. During the Mesozoic Era – the time dinosaurs walked the Earth – the type of plants available to eat changed a lot. Dinosaur dynasties rose and fell according to the plants they ate.

As one type of plant became rare, so the dinosaurs that ate it starved. As another plant took hold and spread around the land, so the dinosaurs that ate that became more numerous.

At the beginning of the Mesozoic Era the most common plants were conifers, such as redwoods and pines, and horse-tails and cycads. Their leaves and seeds were low in calories and difficult to digest. But by the Cretaceous Period, flowering plants, such as sycamores, magnolias and laurels had appeared and thrived. These were much more nutritious, and grew in much greater numbers. The availability of such a rich supply of food meant that in the Cretaceous Period there were more dinosaurs than ever before.

Each type of plant-eating dinosaur had its own way of feeding and dealing with the meat eaters that preyed upon it. The biggest dinosaurs ever were plant eaters. Unlike most meat eaters, many plant eaters walked on all fours. Their teeth were usually flat, to strip and chew the plants they ate.

DINOSAUR FOOD CHAIN

Without plants there would have been no plant-eating dinosaurs. Without them, the meat eaters would have had nothing to eat, either. This process is called a food chain, and the panel below shows an example of one:

Meat eaters (Secondary Consumers) *Spinosaurus*
Plant eaters (Primary Consumers) *Iguanodon*
Plants (Producers) Fern

EARLY HERDS

Plateosaurus was one of the earliest known plant-eating dinosaurs. It travelled in large herds, searching for conifers and ferns in Europe during the Late Triassic Period. Its long neck helped it to reach the leaves that smaller plant eaters left behind. It could probably rear up on its back legs to nibble even higher. It had sharp teeth to break up the tough leaves it ate and probably swallowed stones to help it grind up the food in its stomach. *Plateosaurus* had small claws on its limbs, but its main defence against predators was probably its huge size – it grew to around 7 metres (23 feet).

REACH FOR THE SKY

The tallest dinosaur found so far was *Brachiosaurus*. Towering at about 12.5 metres (40 feet) above the ground, *Brachiosaurus* ate from the tops of tall trees, pulling off leaves with its 52 chisel-shaped teeth. It swallowed its food without chewing, leaving the entire process of digestion to its massive gut. It belonged to an order of dinosaurs called sauropods – the largest land animals to have ever lived. Its fossil remains, dating from the Late Jurassic Period, have been found in North America and Africa. Unlike most plant eaters, whose lives were constantly threatened by meat-eating predators, the *Brachiosaurus* could probably graze in peace, as it was well over twice the size of the largest predators around.

Brachiosaurus

As well as eating vegetation high above the ground, *Brachiosaurus* may have swung its head from side to side, cutting off ground-level plants like a lawn mower.

Even the sharp horns of *Triceratops* would not have saved it from the massive jaws and razor-sharp teeth of *Tyrannosaurus*.

BEAK-FACE

Triceratops was a type of dinosaur called a ceratopsian, meaning "one with a horn". Such dinosaurs existed towards the end of the Cretaceous Period. They lived in much of North America and central Asia. Ceratopsians owed their success to the way they ate. With a sharp, parrot-shaped beak of a mouth, chopping teeth and powerful jaws, they could eat even the toughest plants. They chewed their food, too, making it easier to digest. Like many plant eaters, *Triceratops* was probably a herd animal. It may have travelled large distances in search of food.

Triceratops had a huge skull, with three horns and a bony neck plate. These were its greatest defence against meat eaters. But even its size could not frighten off its chief enemy, *Tyrannosaurus rex*.

Triceratops

Tyrannosaurus rex

SUIT OF ARMOUR

Some plant eaters were heavily armoured. *Saichana* was built like a tank. It was a type of plant eater called an anklyosaur. This one lived around Mongolia during the Late Cretaceous Period.

Saichana's low stooping posture suggests it was a grazer, and it probably nibbled at grasses and bushes with its beak-like mouth. It had a bony plate inside its mouth which allowed it to chew up even the toughest plants.

As well as their fearsome set of body armour, anklyosaurs also had a lethal bony club on the end of their tail to protect them from attackers. The armour must have worked, as anklyosaurs were numerous around North America and East Asia.

Saichana's name means "beautiful lizard". It was called this because of its ornate body armour.

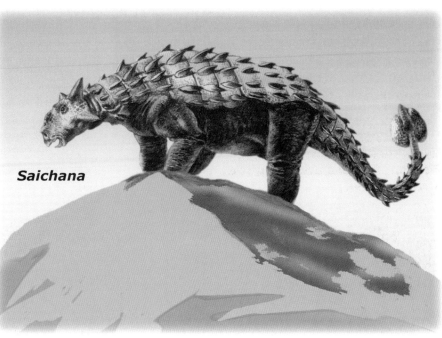

Saichana

Triceratops's skull made up about one-third of its entire length. Experts think that it may have used its long horns to bend down branches to bring them within reach of its mouth.

SPIKES AND PLATES

Other plant eaters had different forms of defence. *Stegosaurus* had its own built-in protection. Its bony back plates were probably too fragile to act effectively as armour, but the spikes on its tail could have been very useful against any attacker.

Stegosaurus lived in North America in the Late Jurassic Period. They weighed 2 tonnes (2 tons), and were at least 6 metres (20 feet) long. Unusually, their back legs were twice as long as their front legs, so their heads sloped forwards towards the ground. The back legs were probably strong enough to allow *Stegosaurus* to rear up to feed on tree branches.

Stegosaurus had a toothless beak at the front of its jaw, with small chewing teeth at the back, to help it mash up the tough ferns, mosses and conifers it ate.

NEW TEETH FOR OLD

One group of dinosaurs, called hadrosaurs, had no teeth at the front of their mouth, but had rows of cheek teeth in their upper and lower jaws. Old teeth, worn out by endlessly chewing a tough plant diet, were continually replaced by new ones. No other type of dinosaur had this natural advantage, and it helped the hadrosaurs become some of the most

ROCK CAKES

Many dinosaurs swallowed stones. These lodged in their stomachs and helped them grind up the tough plant food they ate. Many birds and reptiles still do this today. Such stones are called gastroliths.

common, successful dinosaurs of their time.

Hypacrosaurus was a 9-metre- (30-foot-) long hadrosaur, and it grazed in herds in the forests of North America, during the Late Cretaceous Period. It probably moved on all fours as it searched for pine needles, fruit and magnolia leaves. But unlike most other plant eaters, if threatened it could run away at some speed on its powerful back legs. *Hypacrosaurus* ate all sorts of plants, as the period it lived in saw a huge spread in plant life across the globe. Their success as a species may well have led to the extinction of other plant eaters, such as *Iguanodon*, and giant sauropods, such as *Brachiosaurus*, which were too slow to compete with them.

In the Cretaceous Period, the first trees and flowering plants appeared. Ferns, conifers and gingkoes were still plentiful.

Built for Fighting

Any animal that eats meat has a natural advantage over a plant eater. Meat is the most nutritious food of all and it is easy to digest. A large meal can keep a carnivore going for days before it needs to eat again.

But meat eaters use up a lot of energy to catch a meal. They have to track down their food, then they have to fight it. Their prey may escape, or they themselves may be fatally wounded during the struggle to kill it. While they eat, they may be chased off by larger carnivores, eager for an easy meal. Even worse, unless they are the largest carnivores of all, they may even be hunted and eaten by other predators.

With all these problems, surprise attack and fearsome weaponry were essential for carnivores to survive. Meat-eating dinosaurs had the sharpest brains, the keenest senses, (fossil records show carnivores had noticeably larger areas of their brains controlling sight and smell), and most of all, they had the sharpest teeth and claws.

SHARK-TOOTH KILLER

Tyrannosaurus rex may have ruled the Cretaceous landscape of North America and Asia, but *Carcharodontosaurus* (its name means "Shark-tooth lizard") was the top predator in Africa at that time.

The massive head and jaws of *Tarbosaurus*, a Late Cretaceous predator.

Along with other gigantic theropods, such as *Allosaurus*, *Carcharodontosaurus* was blessed with the most ferocious weapon of all – a skull around 2 metres (6 feet) long, with a massive mouth stuffed to bursting with narrow, curved, serrated-edged teeth. Such teeth made perfect tools for both killing and feeding. Once contact had been made, powerful jaw muscles clamped the teeth tight around the target, and the *Carcharodontosaurus*'s thick neck would jerk backwards and forwards, wrenching huge chunks of flesh away from its victim. As if this wasn't enough, such giant killers had ferocious claws on their hind legs, which could cause lethal wounds to any plant eater. The small front limbs had claws, too.

Although it could run fast on its powerful back legs, the size of *Carcharodontosaurus* and its cousins probably meant a long chase was out of the question. They probably lay in wait for their prey, then dashed out to ambush it. Rushing forward with open mouth, at a speed of around 30 kph (20 mph), they would have aimed at their victim's weakest spot – probably the back of the neck.

GANG WARFARE

Smaller meat eaters could hunt lizards and small mammals alone, but together they could bring down a dinosaur over ten times their own weight. Their hunting techniques may have been similar to those of today's lions and jackals, which create diversions and ambushes to bring down their prey. Then again, perhaps *Deinonychus* just attacked together, hoping to bring down plant-eating prey by sheer ferocity and weight of numbers. Like *Carcharodontosaurus*, *Deinonychus* had a large head filled with sharp teeth. It also had three spindly claws on each hand, and a ferocious 13-centimetre- (5-inch-) long dagger among the claws on its feet.

This illustration is based on an actual fossil find in Montana, USA. The fossil remains show a *Tenontosaurus* alongside several *Deinonychus* – brought down as they tried to overcome the massive plant eater.

Deinonychus

Tenontosaurus

Built for Defence

The big plant eaters had two major problems. The first was finding enough to eat. Plant food is low in nutrition, and a plant-eating animal as big as a dinosaur probably spent almost every waking hour trying to eat enough vegetation to keep it alive. The second problem was being eaten by the most ferocious, terrifying creatures that ever walked the Earth. To cope with this, many plant eaters were well protected, with horns, claws, spikes and armour. Others grew to extreme sizes – becoming the biggest land animals to ever exist. Others, still, were fast enough to run away from trouble. Plant eaters, such as the hadrosaurs and ceratopsians were herd animals, like wildebeest and antelope are today. The herd would have offered safety in numbers, and also allowed most to feed whilst a few kept an eye out for predators.

ARMOUR PLATES

Euoplocephalus was a short and stocky type of dinosaur called an ankylosaur. Covered with heavy bands of armour plates and spikes, it was almost completely protected from above. Thick spines protected the side of its face, and even its eyelids were armoured. But underneath, its softer underbelly was much more vulnerable. To turn it over, a predator had to brave a deadly weapon. Like all ankylosaurs, it had a solid ball of bone at the tip of its tail. Swung round forcefully, it could crush the legs or ribs of an attacker, leaving them with massive internal injuries or broken limbs.

Such powerful defences, together with an ability to eat most kinds of plants, meant that ankylosaurs, such as *Euoplocephalus*, were able to thrive in great numbers.

Euoplocephalus

**Despite its heavy armour,
Euoplocephalus was able
to move fairly quickly
when being chased.**

Tuojiangosaurus

Yangchuanosaurus

The four tail spikes were *Tuojiangosaurus*'s only defense against attacking predators.

VICIOUS TAIL

Threatened by a ravenous meat eater such as *Yangchuanosaurus*, a *Tuojiangosaurus* could defend itself with its four-pronged tail. These bony spikes were well over 0.7 metres (2 feet) long, and could easily inflict a fatal injury if they pierced a predator's innards.

Attack was the *Tuojiangosaurus*'s main means of defence. It was too heavy and lumbering to escape by running away. Its small brain and low intelligence, and the fact that it spent most of its waking life with its head down, grazing the grass, meant that it must have been particularly easy to stalk.

Its 15 pairs of bony back plates might have offered some protection, too. But dinosaur experts are not sure about the use of the spikes and plates found on the backs of stegosaurs like *Tuojiangosaurus*. They certainly look sharp and dangerous enough to put off an attacker, but may have been quite fragile. If this is the case they would have been used mainly to threaten rival males and impress females.

HORNS AND PLATES

The *Styracosaurus* was a ceratopsian – one of the most successful types of plant eaters of the Cretaceous Period. Like the ankylosaurs, their abundance was based on a winning combination of efficient eating habits and ferocious defences. *Styracosaurus* was not as well armoured as the ankylosaurs, but perhaps this made it faster. However, its neck, often one of the most vulnerable spots in any plant eater, was extremely well defended. It had a heavy armour plate, topped with a collar of vicious spikes. The great nose horn would have been very effective, too. Being the wrong end of a charging 5 tonne (5 ton) *Styracosaurus* would be a disastrous experience for even the largest carnivore.

The Way they Walked

Dinosaurs walked in one of two ways. Some walked on their hind legs. These are known as bipeds. Some walked on all four limbs. These are known as quadrupeds. Some two-legged dinosaurs spent time grazing on all fours, but ran on their hind legs.

Dinosaurs developed a way of walking which was far superior to the way their reptilian relatives walk now. Look at any lizard or crocodile, and you can see that their limbs are attached to the sides of their bodies. Some can move incredibly fast, but their muscles have to work extra hard to do this.

Dinosaurs, on the other hand, had their legs directly under their bodies, like birds and mammals do today. This gave them two distinct advantages. The two-legged ones could run faster, and the four-legged ones could carry their weight more easily.

Struthiomimus

A SURVIVOR

Alamosaurus was one of the last of the massive sauropods. It still roamed the Earth at the time of the great dinosaur extinction at the end of the Cretaceous Period. It was named after an American fort defended to the last man against the Mexican army in 1836.

Struthiomimus had to be quick and agile to catch the small, fast-moving prey on which it fed.

Alamosaurus

The large sauropod dinosaurs, such as *Alamosaurus*, *Apatosaurus* and *Diplodocus*, were not designed to move quickly.

SPEED KILLS

Almost every meat-eating dinosaur walked on its hind legs. From the huge *Tyrannosaurus*, right down to the chicken-like *Compsognathus*, carnivores had to chase – and that meant outrunning their prey.

The ostrich-like *Struthiomimus* darted around the riverbanks of Late Cretaceous North America, snapping up small animals and insects. Its long, light legs, driven by powerful thigh and hip muscles, could run at over 50 kph (30 mph).

Struthiomimus's foot, like the feet of all meat-eating dinosaurs, was held so that it was always balanced on its toes. This increased the length of its legs, giving it a longer stride.

HEAVYWEIGHT CHAMPIONS

Anything that weighs over 30 tonnes (30 tons), and is nearly 21 metres (70 feet) long needs a lot of support. Plant eaters, such as *Alamosaurus* had no option but to walk on four legs, and they were superbly designed to do so.

Most plant eaters needed very big stomachs, to digest the huge amount of food they ate. This is one reason why *Alamosaurus* grew so big. Its body was held on four stout elephant-like legs, which were designed to carry its weight rather than allow it to move quickly. Each leg ended in a set of stubby toes, supported by a thick heel pad.

Not all plant eaters walked on four legs, but almost all the four-legged dinosaurs were plant eaters. *Alamosaurus* could probably rear up on its hind legs to reach the very tops of trees. It would have used its long tail as a "fifth leg" to steady its balance.

Brains and Intelligence

If anyone knows one fact about dinosaur intelligence, it is usually "they had brains the size of a walnut". Some of them did, but that did not stop them from being extremely successful animals and thriving on the Earth for millions of years. While it is true that dinosaurs were not the most intelligent of animals, they had the brains they needed to survive.

Much of what we do know about dinosaur brains is based very much on guesswork. Brain and nerve tissue decay very quickly after death, and ideas about dinosaurs' intelligence are based on the size of brain cases and nerve channels in fossilized skulls and backbones. Even this kind of research has only been carried out in around 5 per cent of all known dinosaur types.

Tröodon's large eyes and brain were the secret of its success as a hunter, enabling it to catch small scuttling mammal and lizard prey that would have eluded less intelligent dinosaurs with poorer sight.

On average, dinosaur intelligence can probably be compared with that of bony fish, amphibians, such as frogs, and reptiles, such as crocodiles. What we do know is that the meat eaters had bigger brains than the plant eaters. The more an animal had to do, the more brain power it needed to do it. There is also some evidence, based on what we know about how the brain works, that meat eaters had a more highly developed sense of vision, and plant eaters had a more highly developed sense of smell.

BUSY BRAIN

Tröodon is considered to be the most intelligent of all dinosaurs. Scientists have worked this out by comparing its brain size to the rest of its body. It was probably smarter than an average emu, and at least as clever as a possum. Its way of life required a lot of brain power. Large grasping hands, with slim fingers would have allowed it to be able to grasp and pull. It was very fast on its feet and could probably move with great agility. Studies of the brain case suggest that it had a good sense of balance. It also had very large eyes for a dinosaur, and may even have been a night hunter.

Kentrosaurus

Heavily armoured and with little more to concentrate on than munching leaves, *Kentrosaurus* had no need of a large brain.

Tröodon

NOT VERY SMART

Scientists work out dinosaur intelligence by comparing the size of a dinosaur's brain with the size of its body. This is called the "Encephalization Quotient" (EQ). They match the dinosaur EQ with the EQ of living animals such as fish, crocodiles and small mammals and assume their intelligence to be similar.

NUT-SIZED BRAIN

Kentrosaurus belongs to the stegosaur family. Its tiny head really did contain a brain the size of a walnut, but this was enough to control its bulky body. Its protective armour plates and spikes meant that it did not need to think quickly when facing an attacker.

Sight and Sound

Little is known about how dinosaurs saw their world and what sort of noises they made. We can make some guesses about their eyesight based on fossil remains of optic nerve channels and brains cases, and on what we know about animals today. Most hunters have sharp colour vision and it is likely that the meat-eating dinosaurs had this, too. Many plant eaters today have quite poor vision and some only see in black and white. Perhaps many plant-eating dinosaurs were like this as well.

There is even less evidence available relating to the sounds that dinosaurs made. But from howling to attract a mate or calling to warn others of danger, to bellowing in fear or snarling in anger, sound is an essential part of the animal world. No doubt dinosaurs made these noises, too.

Tröodon's eyes were large and forward-facing.

STEREOSCOPIC SIGHT

The position of the eye sockets in an animal's skull gives it various advantages and disadvantages. If the eyes are placed squarely on the side of the head, then it is likely that an animal has a good all round view of its surroundings. It can watch pretty much everything around it without even having to move its head. If the eyes are placed more to the front of the head, so that their field of vision overlaps, this all round view is lost. But it is replaced by something much more useful – stereoscopic sight. Fossil skull remains show us that tyrannosaurs such as the *Alioramus*, had this stereoscopic vision. This gives an animal the ability to judge depth – vital for a hunter who needs to time a surprise ambush to the split second, or judge a leap on to the back of a ceratopsian precisely, to avoid its lethal horns.

Head crest of
Parasaurolophus

An adult male's crest was about 1 metre (3 feet) long. Females and young Parasaurolophus had smaller crests.

A snort from the nostrils caused air inside the crest's tubes to vibrate and make a low hooting sound. Animals of different sizes would produce different notes.

Bony tubes

Nostril opening

Brain cavity

At first, scientists thought that the crest might have been used like a snorkel when the dinosaur fed on underwater plants. But this could not have been the case because the tubes are sealed at the end, not open.

Eye socket

Lower jaw

Teeth for grinding up plant food.

Parasaurolophus had a long, hollow, backward-curving crest on top of its skull. It used its crest to call to other Parasaurolophuses. It had two nasal sacs that it inflated when it was about to call.

MUSICAL CRESTS

Some of the plant-eating hadrosaurs had curious crests and crescents on their heads. Many theories have been put forward regarding their use, from breathing apparatus to mating displays. The most likely one is that they generated sound. Inside the crest of the *Parasaurolophus*, were a series of passages. Recent research with a reconstructed crest has shown that this would have made a great, deep, reverberating note. Such a noise would have travelled long distances over the forests of Late Cretaceous North America, where *Parasaurolophus* made its home. Perhaps *Parasaurolophus* made such noises to make contact with others of its kind. (Whales are able to communicate over vast distances today, using similar low frequency sounds.) Deep notes are also ideal as a warning, since it is difficult to identify where they came from. This would be essential for any plant eater not wanting to draw attention to itself from a predator on the prowl.

ABLE TO SEE IN THE DARK

During the Mesozoic Era dinosaurs lived in the Antarctic region of the Earth. Although it was warmer than it is today, there were still long periods of continuous darkness during the winter. Fossil evidence shows that animals such as *Leaellynasaura* who lived there, had especially well developed eyes to help them see during these dark days.

Colour

Nobody knows what colour dinosaurs were. Their bones may remain with us as fossils. The texture of their skin may imprint itself in mud which turns to rock. Even their footprints have left their mark in the Earth. But colour is something that has not survived the 70 million-year gap between extinction and today.

When the Victorians first became aware of dinosaurs in mid-nineteenth century Britain, they thought that the gigantic creatures they found would have been a dull green, brown or grey. These were the colours of the largest animals, such as elephants, or reptiles, such as crocodiles or monitor lizards, which their dinosaur finds slightly resembled.

Today, we are not so sure. Much of what we imagine dinosaurs looked like is based on what we know about animals now. Animals survive and thrive because they have specific features, or adaptations, which give them some natural advantage in the world they inhabit. Some,

including dinosaur descendants, such as birds, snakes and lizards, use colours as camouflage, warning signals and to communicate with each other. The colours in this book are based on successful colour adaptations seen in animals today.

Camouflage

Prosaurolophus grazed and foraged for pine needles, magnolia leaves, seeds and fruits in the Cretaceous forests of North America. Its likely colouring may have reflected the dark, shaded world of the forest floor. Browny and dark- and light-green patches would help it blend among the tree trunks, leaves and shafts of sunlight.

It is thought that many hadrosaurs like *Prosaurolophus* had this kind of coloration. And it was not only plant eaters that had such markings. The stalking carnivores had just as much need to hide themselves from their prey, and many were probably coloured in this way, too.

A *Stegosaurus* flushes its back plates bright pink to scare off a threatening *Allosaurus*.

DON'T MAKE ME ANGRY!

Imagine this scene: an *Allosaurus* approaches a *Stegosaurus* and they circle each other, ready for a fight to the death. As they roar and snarl, the *Stegosaurus* flushes its diamond-shaped back plates bright pink, sending an alarm signal to its enemy.

Many animals today use a similar tactic – called a "threat display" – to avoid a real fight. The idea is to show your opponent that you are extremely angry and prepared to do battle. When it was courting female *Stegosauruses*, a male probably also flushed its plates at rival males, to warn them off.

This is still just a theory. Research has suggested that the plates on *Stegosaurus's* back were too fragile to be much use as armour.

With its colouring helping it to blend in with its forest surroundings, *Prosaurolophus* could forage safely, hidden from predators.

They were also rich in blood vessels, which could have made the plates flush pink. Like predators today, *Allosaurus* probably had sharp colour vision. Instinct or experience would have warned it that a *Stegosaurus* with bright pink spines was likely to put up a fight.

TOO BIG TO BOTHER

The biggest dinosaurs were probably dull browns, greens or greys, as the Victorians thought. Once an animal reaches a certain size, camouflage becomes useless. It is too big to hide, and it is also unlikely to be attacked for the same reason.

Eggs and Nests

Eggs had lumpy surfaces to stop them bunching together in the nest.

Some dinosaur babies were able to look after themselves immediately after birth – others were not.

Eggs were often arranged in groups in the nest.

This illustration is based directly on that most rare of dinosaur finds – an actual egg with an embyro inside it.

Egg shells had tiny pores to allow the babies to breathe.

A few dinosaurs gave birth to live young, but most dinosaurs laid eggs. The eggs and nests that have been found have much to tell us about how dinosaurs lived. Like most reptiles today, dinosaurs had many young, but did not usually look after them. Only a few seem to have nurtured their babies once they had hatched.

There have been no egg finds for whole dinosaur families, such as the stegosaurs and ankylosaurs. But what we do know is very revealing. Communal egg sites tell us that the dinosaurs who made them were sociable. Massive nesting sites tell us that, like birds, some dinosaurs returned to the same spot year after year to lay their eggs.

Some nests were carefully constructed. They had leaf linings, or earth rims. The eggs inside were often laid and arranged with care. But other eggs were laid as the dinosaur walked along, absent mindedly depositing her offspring in the tracks behind her. (Chameleons still do this today.)

BABY FACE

Fossil evidence reveals that in one dinosaur family, the hadrosaurs, the young looked noticeably different from the adults. They had all the classic, cute baby features of big eyes, round heads and shortened snouts, that scientists think trigger nurturing instincts in animal parents.

INSIDE THE EGG

Curled up snugly, an *Orodromeus* baby grows inside its egg. Eggs were often one of as many as 19, laid in a carefully arranged spiral, by a small, two-legged plant eater. Typical vertebrate eggs had a hard shell which let gases in and out. This would enable the growing dinosaur inside to take in oxygen. When the baby was ready to hatch, it was also ready for the outside world. *Orodromeus* hatchlings entered the world fully able to look after themselves. Their parents may have guarded the unhatched eggs, but would not have looked after the babies.

We know this because nest finds show eggs that have opened but remained untrampled. This shows that the baby left the nest immediately. Whether it discovered its new world in the relative safety of a small clutch of other baby *Orodromeus*, or struck out alone, we do not know.

HELLO, MUM

A female *Leaellynasaura* stoops over her hungry hatchlings. As they chirp for food, she spits out a nourishing paste of half-digested plant food. The nests were hollowed in the ground and lined with insulating leaves. They generated warmth as they decayed, and kept the eggs at a temperature necessary for the life within them to flourish.

The babies would have been around 30 centimetres (1 foot) when they hatched, and were totally dependent on their parents. Their bones were too weak to allow much movement, so they would have had to be fed in their nest.

We know that some dinosaur babies were like this because nest finds have shown egg shells trampled into small pieces. One find showed a nest full of babies. The instinct to stay must have been very strong, because they all died there. Perhaps a parent was killed while foraging for food to bring back for them, and the abandoned chicks starved to death.

Unusually for dinosaurs, *Leaellynasauras* invested a lot of care and attention on both their nests and their hatchlings.

Feet and Footprints

During their life on Earth dinosaurs evolved extremely effective ways of getting about. From the speedy two-legged meat eaters to the huge four-legged plant eaters, all of them walked on their toes. This did not necessarily make them as graceful, but it did mean that they could move their bodies with minimum effort and maximum efficiency.

These feet also left the only evidence, aside from eggs and teeth marks, of what dinosaurs actually did during their lifetimes. Dinosaur tracks were first found in 1836, but it took a while for science to realize the importance of this discovery. It is difficult to believe that something as fleeting as a footprint could survive for the 65 million years or more since the dinosaurs became extinct. But survive they did, and dinosaur footprints have much to tell us about their owners.

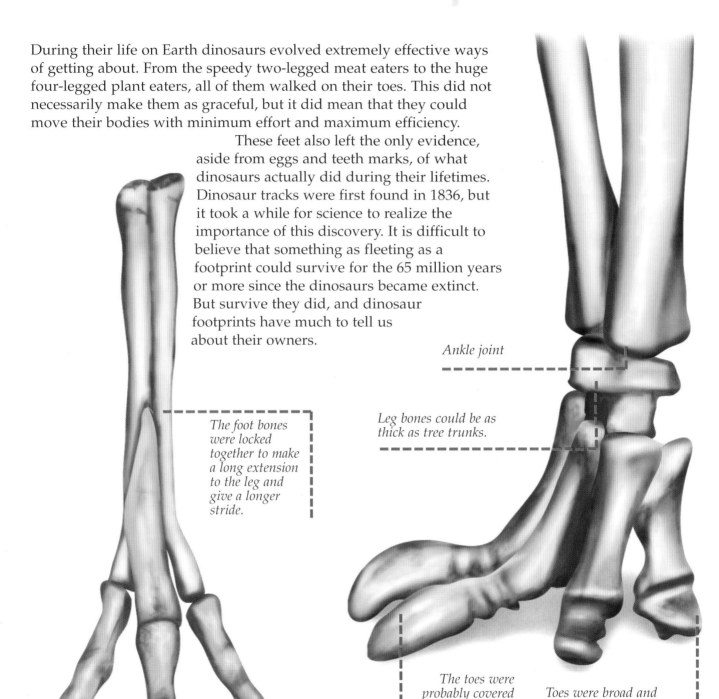

Ankle joint

Leg bones could be as thick as tree trunks.

The foot bones were locked together to make a long extension to the leg and give a longer stride.

The toes were probably covered by round, horny pads.

Toes were broad and splayed to spread the weight over a wide area.

Birdlike toes

Sharp claws

The feet of two-legged theropod carnivores (left) were built for speed and balance, while those of four-legged sauropod herbivores (above) were designed to support the dinosaur's great body weight.

46

TWO TYPES OF FEET

There are two different types of dinosaur feet (shown left). The bone structure of these two types gives a lot of information about how dinosaurs moved around. The first foot belongs to a two-legged, or bipedal, theropod predator. The long, slender, birdlike toes gave a solid grip on the ground and kept the animal as well balanced as possible—all vital skills in the acrobatic twists and turns of a chase. Walking on toes also increased the length of the leg, so this dinosaur would have had a longer stride. This meant that it could walk or run faster.

The second foot belongs to a four-legged, or quadrupedal, sauropod plant eater. It had to hold and transport a huge amount of weight, and is remarkably similar to the foot of a modern-day elephant. The toes were shorter and broader than in the theropod foot. Although the dinosaur walked on its toes, the hind foot was supported by a thick, fibrous wedge, which acted like the heel of a shoe. Like elephants do today, sauropods probably walked with their legs held stiffly. This wedge would have saved them the effort of having to lift the entire foot off the ground whenever they took a step.

DINOSAUR FARMERS

Because of their enormous weight, dinosaur footprints did much to churn up the soil and vegetation where they walked. Such disruption to the local environment would have created ideal conditions for the new flowering plants of the Cretaceous Period to take root and flourish.

Apatosaurus footprints left in riverbank mud

OUT FOR A STROLL

A group of *Apatosauruses* trek across the soft mud of a riverbank, one misty Late Jurassic morning. Although they are difficult to read very accurately, the tracks dinosaurs left behind give us some clues about their appearance and habits. For example, the deep indentations left by these *Apatosauruses* give a strong impression of great weight. The sets of tracks are side by side, suggesting they were sociable, herd animals. Tracks left in mud flats, sand dunes, and swamps have now been found all over the world. Far more meat eater tracks have been discovered than plant eater tracks. This is almost certainly because meat eaters were much more active than plant eaters, and probably spent much of their lives patrolling their territory searching for prey.

Teeth

The teeth increased in size from the back of the jaw to the front.

Tyrannosaurus's saw-like, backward-curving teeth sliced through flesh and tough dinosaur skin with ease.

Some of the teeth grew up to 18 cm (7 in) long.

Dinosaur teeth tell a fascinating story. They come in all shapes and sizes and show what a dinosaur ate and how it ate it. Killing teeth, tearing teeth, plucking teeth, grinding teeth – all worked to suit the diet and life style of the dinosaur they belonged to.

Dinosaurs were constantly replacing teeth throughout their lives. This is something reptiles and some other animals still do today. The plant eaters ground down their teeth with their endless chewing, and the meat eaters left teeth in the corpses of their victims.

Some dinosaurs, such as the ornithomimids did not even have teeth. They had a sharp, beak-like mouth which was well-adapted to their omnivorous (plant- and meat-eating) diet. Other dinosaurs, such as the plant-eating hadrosaurs, had over a thousand teeth packed into their jaws.

With its fearsome array of sharp teeth and powerful jaw muscles, *Tyrannosaurus* held its prey in a vice-like grip. Then it simply twisted its head to rip off a chunk of meat.

OUCH!

As you might expect, the carnivore *Tyrannosaurus rex* had a skull full of ferocious bone-crunching and flesh-tearing teeth. Other top predators in the dinosaur world had teeth with many similar features. The sharp, cone-shaped spikes were ideally suited to the task of killing and eating the hadrosaurs and ceratopsians that they hunted. Designed to aid the *Tyrannosaurus* in a quick kill, the curved teeth would sink further into struggling prey, making escape or fighting back even more unlikely.

The teeth were attached to a heavily-built jaw that was over 1.2 metres (4 feet) long. The jaw was even hinged at the top of the skull to allow the snout to tilt up and down. This would absorb the shock of the first killing bite, and allow the *Tyrannosaurus* some flexibility while feeding. The jaw had some give at the sides, too, and could bulge out, to accommodate a particularly large mouthful of meat.

Tyrannosaurus shared many features of its teeth with another terrifying predator – today's shark. Not only were the teeth replaceable, but they were also serrated, like a kitchen carving knife. This was particularly useful when it came to tearing off huge chunks of meat.

SLICE UP

Ceratopsians such as *Triceratops* probably benefited from the most efficient plant-eating apparatus. Well-muscled jaws like these could cope with a wide variety of plant food, from the toughest cones and branches, to the more succulent and easily-digested flowering plants. There was certainly plenty of choice in the *Triceratops's* habitat – the upland forests of North America.

FULL STOMACH

Not all plant eaters relied on their teeth to eat. Some, such as the huge sauropods, just used their teeth to strip leaves from trees, and did not chew their food before they swallowed. They relied entirely on their huge stomachs to break up their food.

Triceratops's **beak got worn down by tough plants, but it continued to grow during the dinosaur's life.**

The sharp, horny beak was used to snip up tough leaves, stems and branches.

The teeth were self-sharpening

The front part of the jaw, a parrot-like beak, was designed for cutting. Behind the beak were hundreds of sharp, interlocking teeth, which moved up and down like guillotine blades, slicing up vegetation as the *Triceratops* chewed. Its large muscular tongue would push its food between its cheeks and teeth, before swallowing and further digestion in the stomach.

Skin

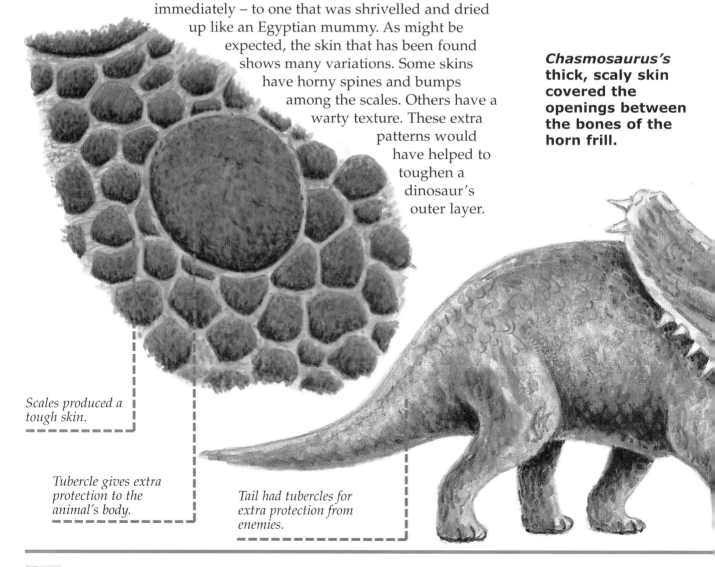

We can take a good guess at what sort of shape dinosaurs were from the bones they left behind. Put together, like a huge jigsaw puzzle, the bones also tell us how big they were. But what did they look like on the outside? Although we can only guess at their colour, we do have a little more idea about what their skin was like. Over the years, some remarkable fossils have come to light, which have preserved the texture of dinosaur skin. They show quite clearly that dinosaurs had a scaly reptilian surface, much like the hide of a crocodile today.

But a few skin imprints on mud that has turned to stone, can never tell the whole story – especially in a class of animals as wide-ranging as the dinosaurs. Because they are so delicate, fossil skin impressions are very difficult to find and preserve. We also have no idea at what stage of an animal's decay the impression was made. An imprint could be anything – from a dinosaur that died and was preserved almost immediately – to one that was shrivelled and dried up like an Egyptian mummy. As might be expected, the skin that has been found shows many variations. Some skins have horny spines and bumps among the scales. Others have a warty texture. These extra patterns would have helped to toughen a dinosaur's outer layer.

Cetiosaurus's thick skin would not have protected it from predators such as **Stegosaurus**.

Chasmosaurus's thick, scaly skin covered the openings between the bones of the horn frill.

Scales produced a tough skin.

Tubercle gives extra protection to the animal's body.

Tail had tubercles for extra protection from enemies.

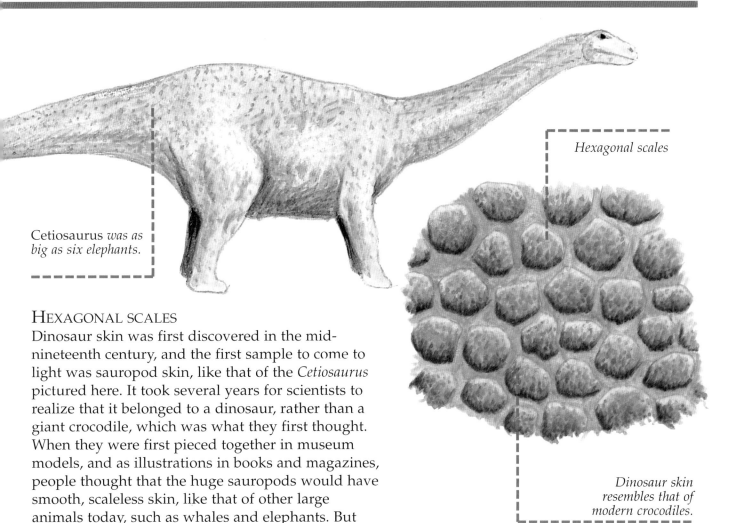

Cetiosaurus *was as big as six elephants.*

Hexagonal scales

Dinosaur skin resembles that of modern crocodiles.

HEXAGONAL SCALES

Dinosaur skin was first discovered in the mid-nineteenth century, and the first sample to come to light was sauropod skin, like that of the *Cetiosaurus* pictured here. It took several years for scientists to realize that it belonged to a dinosaur, rather than a giant crocodile, which was what they first thought. When they were first pieced together in museum models, and as illustrations in books and magazines, people thought that the huge sauropods would have smooth, scaleless skin, like that of other large animals today, such as whales and elephants. But the reptilian, hexagonal scales on the skin clearly showed that this was not the case. More recent fossil finds suggest that some sauropods may also have had spines along the skin of their backs, like the fringes on iguanas.

LUMPS AND BUMPS

Fossil skin samples of a ceratopsian called *Chasmosaurus* show that, not only does it have scales, but it also has bumps placed among them.

These bumps, known as tubercles, would add an additional protective covering to the hide, and may have been more numerous around vulnerable areas of a dinosaur's body, such as the neck, thigh and tail. The scales on ceratopsian skin samples have been found to be much larger than scales on iguanodonts, for example. The larger scales would have made the hide thicker and given the dinosaur more protection from the claws and teeth of predators.

KEEP YOUR COOL

Some scientists think that the extra lumps and bumps on dinosaur skin were to give them a greater overall surface area. Because there was more of the body to lose heat from, this would have helped them to stay cooler when it was hot.

Feathers

Fossils of *Sinornithisaurus millenii* seem to show that some dinosaurs had feathers, probably for insulation.

During the mid-nineteenth century, scientists realized that birds and reptiles shared some characteristics. Ever since then, people have wondered whether these two types of animal also had common ancestors in the dinosaurs. The discovery of *Archaeopteryx* in 1861 added fuel to this debate. *Archaeopteryx* is considered to be the first bird, but its skeleton is strikingly similar to the theropod dinosaur *Compsognathus*.

In the mid-1990s other extraordinary fossil finds, unearthed in China, set dinosaur experts reeling. One dinosaur, named *Sinosauropteryx prima*, was a tiny theropod, around 1 metre (3 feet) long, dating from around 135 million years ago. Like *Archaeopteryx*, this dinosaur was also similar in many ways to *Compsognathus*. But what made it so unusual was the fact that its body was covered in tiny 3-centimetre- (1-inch-) long feathers. The structure of the feathers made them unsuitable for flying, so they probably acted as insulation. This discovery was important evidence for the argument that birds were descended from small dinosaurs who had evolved feathers. Such fossil-finds are making us re-think our ideas about what dinosaurs looked like, particularly the meat-eating theropods.

Long dinosaur-like tail

Sinornithosaurus millenii *had strong back legs because it could not fly.*

Wing-like upper arms

Sinornithosaurus millenii

NEXT STOP, BIRDS?

Protarchaeopteryx, which dates from the same period as *Sinosauropteryx prima*, is thought to be another ancestor of *Archaeopteryx*. It had a bird-like appearance. Although it could not fly, its bones were hollow, and it had sprouted feathers instead of scales. Most of its body was covered in short, downy feathers, but it had longer feathers on its front limbs and tail. Like other early, bird-like dinosaurs, the feathers were intended to keep it warm. This also suggests that this dinosaur was warm-blooded, like its bird descendants. Two other recent finds, named *Sinornithosaurus millenii* (see left), and *Archaeoraptor liaoningensis*, also resemble a curious half-way house between dinosaurs and birds. Fossil remains show clear evidence of feathers, and they both have wing-like upper limbs, and lightweight hollow bones. But they also have long dinosaur tails, and could almost certainly not fly.

It was many millions of years before the feathers that had originally evolved to keep their owners warm were used for gliding, and eventually, powered flight. But it is feathers, more than any other physical characteristic, that make birds the greatest flyers in the animal world.

Tyrannosaurus's *whole body may have been covered in feathers.*

Short arms *were typical of* Tyrannosaurus rex.

Feathers are thought *to have been more "shaggy" than birds' feathers.*

Tyrannosaurus rex baby

It is possible that a newly hatched baby *Tyrannosaurus* had a fluffy down covering, which it would gradually shed as it grew bigger.

FLUFFY T-REX!

The tough-guy image of the *Tyrannosaurus rex* has taken a serious bashing. Fossil-finds suggest that tyrannosaur hatchlings may have been covered in downy feathers, much like those of baby birds. Many of *Tyrannosaurus's* relatives had feathers, so it may have had them, too. If the adult did have feathers though, they would have been used to attract the attention of a mate, rather than to keep warm. Large animals, such as the *Tyrannosaurus,* had little need for the extra insulation that feathers would bring, especially in the warm, humid environment in which they lived. But baby animals lose heat from their bodies much more quickly, and need to be kept warm.

Dinosaur Blood

All animals are either warm- or cold-blooded. Cold-blooded animals, such as reptiles, have bodies which are as warm or cold as their surroundings. Warm and cold weather affects them more than warm-blooded animals. If they are too cold they become slow. If they are too hot, they dry up and die.

Warm-blooded animals, such as birds and mammals, burn up food to make their own heat in their bodies. They have to stay the same temperature, no matter what their environment is like.

Dromiceiomimus

Dromiceiomimus is one of the dinosaurs that has been used by scientists to prove that dinosaurs were warm-blooded.

Komodo dragon

There are advantages and disadvantages to both systems. For example, warm-blooded animals tend to be more active, but have to eat all the time to keep their bodies going. Cold-blooded animals can make a meal last for weeks. There has been a great deal of discussion about whether dinosaurs were warm-blooded or cold-blooded. No one knows for sure. Dinosaurs themselves could be so completely different – compare a huge four-legged plant eater, such as *Diplodocus*, with a tiny meat eater, such as *Compsognathus* – that it is entirely possible that some were warm-blooded and some were cold-blooded.

WARM-BLOODED THEORY

This *Dromiceiomimus* stalks the forests of Alberta, its keen eyes straining in the dark, looking for any unwary lizard or scurrying mammal foolish enough to think that night-time was a safe time to venture out. Night hunters, such as *Dromiceiomimus* provide one of the arguments for dinosaurs being warm-blooded. The lower temperatures at night would make it much more difficult for a cold-blooded animal to move with any speed and agility.

It is the dinosaurs' fleet-footedness, more than anything else, which makes many people believe that they were warm-blooded. Supporters of this theory also point out that dinosaur hearts were similar in structure to other warm-blooded animals, such as mammals. Finally, they say that birds, who are direct descendants from dinosaurs, are warm-blooded, too.

COLD-BLOODED THEORY

When dinosaur remains were first discovered in the nineteenth century, their similarity to cold-blooded reptiles made people think that they must be cold-blooded too. When it was discovered that dinosaurs evolved from animals who were unquestionably cold-blooded, this argument held even more weight.

Other supporters on the cold-blooded side, point to the *Stegosaurus* and its massive back plates. Cold-blooded animals need to bask in the morning sun before they are warm enough to move around. It has been suggested that these plates were built-in temperature control devices. Turned flat to the sun, they would absorb heat rapidly, letting the *Stegosaurus* quickly reach the correct temperature. When the *Stegosaurus* was too hot, the plates could be turned away from the sun and even aligned in the direction of a cool breeze, to take heat away from its body.

Yet another argument suggests that dinosaurs could still have been as active as they were and been cold-blooded, because they lived in a much warmer climate than we do today. Because they were so huge they would have kept their body heat much longer than smaller animals. So they could have remained lively when it was colder, even though they were cold-blooded.

The Komodo dragon is cold-blooded. Many scientists say that the fact that reptiles today are cold-blooded proves that dinosaurs probably were too.

Dinosaur Bones

MAKING A DIFFERENCE

Not all the features of *Diplodocus* are common to all the giant sauropods. Other huge plant eaters such as *Brachiosaurus* and *Apatosaurus* did not have a hollow bone structure, and were much heavier.

Nothing about dinosaurs has survived quite as well as their bones. And bones tell tales in extraordinary detail. A complete skeleton will give a scientist a good idea of the likely size and appearance of a dinosaur. A skull will reveal what it probably ate, and features such as claws and armour plates will show how it attacked enemies or defended itself.

Its small skull meant less weight for its long neck to carry.

Long neck bones allowed it to reach the very tops of trees.

A single long tendon (shown here in red) stretched from neck to tail along a groove in the backbone, keeping both in balance.

Hollow vertebrae made its skeleton lighter.

Its thigh bone was very straight to give the legs maximum strength to support its heavy weight.

A single clawed toe on each foot was used for defence.

BUILT TO PLOD

Diplodocus dedicated its life to munching leaves off the tops of tall trees. Its body shape reveals how well it was designed to do this. *Diplodocus* was a huge animal – at least 26 metres (85 feet) long. It weighed 10 tonnes (10 tons), surprisingly light for such a large sauropod. Its skeleton did not do all the work. Clever arrangements of muscles also supported its massive frame.

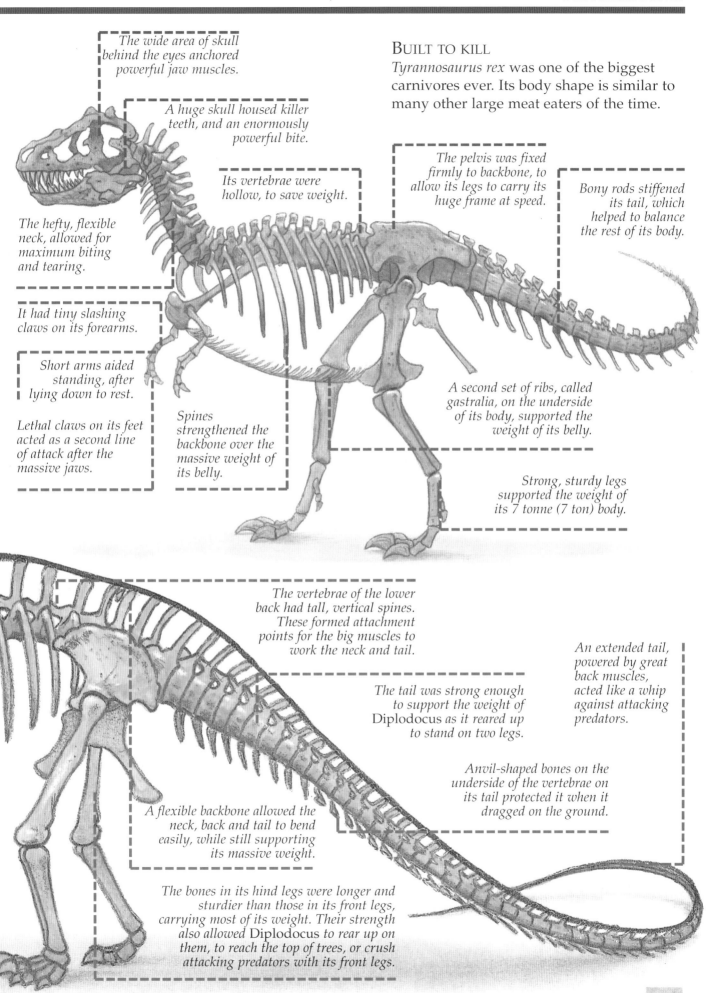

The wide area of skull behind the eyes anchored powerful jaw muscles.

A huge skull housed killer teeth, and an enormously powerful bite.

BUILT TO KILL
Tyrannosaurus rex was one of the biggest carnivores ever. Its body shape is similar to many other large meat eaters of the time.

The pelvis was fixed firmly to backbone, to allow its legs to carry its huge frame at speed.

Its vertebrae were hollow, to save weight.

Bony rods stiffened its tail, which helped to balance the rest of its body.

The hefty, flexible neck, allowed for maximum biting and tearing.

It had tiny slashing claws on its forearms.

Short arms aided standing, after lying down to rest.

Lethal claws on its feet acted as a second line of attack after the massive jaws.

Spines strengthened the backbone over the massive weight of its belly.

A second set of ribs, called gastralia, on the underside of its body, supported the weight of its belly.

Strong, sturdy legs supported the weight of its 7 tonne (7 ton) body.

The vertebrae of the lower back had tall, vertical spines. These formed attachment points for the big muscles to work the neck and tail.

An extended tail, powered by great back muscles, acted like a whip against attacking predators.

The tail was strong enough to support the weight of *Diplodocus* as it reared up to stand on two legs.

Anvil-shaped bones on the underside of the vertebrae on its tail protected it when it dragged on the ground.

A flexible backbone allowed the neck, back and tail to bend easily, while still supporting its massive weight.

The bones in its hind legs were longer and sturdier than those in its front legs, carrying most of its weight. Their strength also allowed *Diplodocus* to rear up on them, to reach the top of trees, or crush attacking predators with its front legs.

When Did the Dinosaurs Die?

Dinosaurs were among the most numerous, long-lived and successful animals the world has ever seen. But about 65 million years ago, something big happened on Earth. It affected global climate, seas, landscape, plants and animals. It was the end of an era–the Mesozoic Era–and the end of the Age of Dinosaurs.

DATING THE CHANGE

Exactly what happened is not clear, although some ideas are shown in this section. But it was enough to mark a clear, rapid, worldwide change or transition in rocks and fossils, between the Cretaceous Period and the Tertiary Period. The transition is called the K-T boundary. K is for kreta meaning chalk, the main rock formed in the Cretaceous Period.

T is for the Tertiary Period. Radio-dating measures the amounts of natural radioactivity in ancient rocks, which change very slowly with time. It puts the K-T boundary at about 65–64.5 million years ago.

MASS EXTINCTION

After the Cretaceous Period there were no more dinosaur fossils. Dinosaurs were not the only creatures to die out during this period. Many other kinds of animals and plants also disappeared from the fossil record. This disappearance of many kinds of living things at around the same time has happened several times during the Earth's history and is known as a mass extinction.

OTHER MASS EXTINCTIONS

The fossil record shows many periods of mass extinctions, especially:

• End of the Cambrian, 505 million years ago.

• End of the Devonian, 360 million years ago.

• Middle and end of the Permian, about 250 million years ago. This was the greatest of all. Many larger animals disappeared, including the sail-backed, pre-dinosaur reptile *Dimetrodon*, as well as lots of land plants. Nine-tenths of ocean life was wiped out, including the last trilobites.

• End of the Cretaceous, as shown here.

The world as it may have looked at the end of the Cretaceous Period.

Dimetrodon **was one of many creatures that became extinct around 250 million years ago.**

WERE DINOSAURS ALREADY DYING OUT? Possibly, depending on where you look. Fossil surveys in different regions give different results. One world survey showed that at any one time during the Age of Dinosaurs, there were at least 50–100 species in 20–30 groups or families, and this dinosaur range continued right to the end of the Cretaceous Period. However, a study of North American fossils suggests that dinosaurs decreased and mammals increased over the last 10 million years of the Cretaceous Period.

Did the Dinosaurs Freeze or Fry?

Every few years a big volcano erupts somewhere on Earth. Vast clouds of smoke and ash blast into the air. They drift around the world, screen out the Sun and affect weather for weeks or months. In June 1991 the eruption of Mount Pinatubo in the Philippines affected the world's climate for about two years.

COLD AND COUGHING

While some scientists believe that a giant meteorite wiped out the dinosaurs, another theory suggests that a series of volcanic eruptions was responsible. But not just from one volcano – from dozens, even hundreds of them. The mass eruptions filled the air with smoke and ash. Dust settled and cloaked plants. Poisonous sulphur fumes choked animals. Vast clouds made midday cool and gloomy. Without light and warmth, plants began to die.

Dinosaurs and other animals who depended on plants began to die, too, coughing and shivering and starving.

DID THE DINOSAURS SUFFOCATE?

If many volcanoes erupted at the end of the Cretaceous Period, they could have used up the oxygen in the air. All living animals must breathe oxygen to survive. Presumably the dinosaurs did, too. Chemical tests have been done on tiny prehistoric air bubbles in lumps of fossil plant resin, amber. Results show how the oxygen in the air fell from 35 per cent about 67 million years ago to 28 per cent 2 million years later. Perhaps the dinosaurs could not get enough air through their small nostrils into their huge bodies to survive and suffocated to death!

This is how some parts of the earth may have looked at the end of the Cretaceous Period.

WHERE WERE THE VOLCANOES?

At the end of the Cretaceous Period there were probably ranges of volcanoes around the West Pacific Ocean and across North America, Greenland and western Europe. But the main region was the vast volcanic region called the Deccan Traps, in what is now India. The Deccan eruptions may have lasted years, even centuries.

GLOBAL WARMING

Another idea is that the volcanoes released the "greenhouse gas" carbon dioxide. This made the atmosphere warmer (as is happening today because of our polluting gases). As the climate heated up, large land animals, such as dinosaurs suffered in the sweltering temperatures. They slowly fried away.

CONTINENTAL DRIFT

The massive volcanic eruptions may have been due to the great earth movements of continental drift. As landmasses moved around the globe and seas changed shape, the world's winds and ocean currents took up new patterns.

PREHISTORIC OZONE HOLE

Sunlight can change the hazy fumes from volcanic eruptions into chemicals that damage the protective ozone layer in our Earth's atmosphere. Without the ozone shield, the Sun's harmful ultraviolet rays reach the surface and cause sunburn, radiation sickness and skin cancer. Did the dinosaurs suffer this fate and burn up at the end of the Cretaceous Period?

This brought rapid climate change. Temperatures at the Equator could have fallen by 5 °C, and in the mid-latitudes by 20 °C. Did cold winters finish off the dinosaurs?

Death from Outer Space

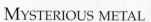

Some experts say that the death of the dinosaurs happened gradually, taking a million years. Others suggest that it was fast, only a few years – maybe triggered by an event that took just a few seconds. The event was a massive lump of rock from outer space, a meteorite or asteroid, that crashed into the Earth. There is some evidence for this idea.

MYSTERIOUS METAL

In some parts of the world, Late Cretaceous rocks are separated from early Tertiary rocks by a layer of red-grey clay about 2 cm (just under 1 inch) thick. Chemical tests show that this clay has up to 30 times the normal amount of iridium, a type of metal. Iridium is rare in most rocks. But it is found in larger amounts at the centre of the Earth – and in meteorites from outer space.

MASSIVE METEORITE!

From the amounts of iridium in the clay, it is calculated the meteorite was about 10 kilometres (6 miles) across – the size of a big town! It was travelling about 20 kilometres (12 miles) every second (70 times faster than a jet plane). It smashed into Earth with the same force as 100 million atomic bombs.

INCREDIBLE IMPACT

The incredible blast from such a meteorite would send sound and shock waves around the world. The impact would instantly heat and vaporize much of the rock from the meteorite and the ground it hit. The smash would also throw up gigantic clouds of spray and dust high into the atmosphere.

WORLDWIDE WINTER

Imagine how the dust cloud spread around the world, blotting out the Sun. It became night for weeks, maybe years. It was dark and cold in the gloom, just like winter. Deprived of light and warmth, plants withered and died.

OTHER RESULTS OF THE IMPACT

- The shock waves from the impact could have triggered fires, volcanic eruptions, earthquakes and tsunamis (tidal waves) around the planet.
- The dust cloud would have disturbed global winds and ocean currents.
- Extra gases in the air would have formed strong acid rain, which would acid-burn plants and animals both on land and at the surface of the sea.

Animals that ate the plants starved. Animals that ate these animals starved, too. In any case cold-blooded animals would be too cool to move. Was this how the dinosaurs met their end?

Other Extinction Theories

Can you think of a weird and wonderful reason why the dinosaurs may have died out? Each time a new discovery is made in science, someone suggests that it killed off the dinosaurs. Sadly most of these theories do not explain why many other animals and plants died with the dinosaurs. Nor do they show why other animals and plants survived.

DANGERS FROM DEEP SPACE?

There are many ideas about how events in space made the dinosaurs extinct:

• Extra-big solar flares. These vast tongues of flaming gas leap from the Sun's surface and give out extra heat and harmful rays.

• A supernova, when a giant star blows itself to bits in a gigantic final explosion. A supernova near Earth could send out deadly rays and magnetic waves to harm life here.

• A smaller star might die by collapsing into a black hole. This would release huge bursts of the atomic particles called neutrinos. They would shower Earth like invisible rain, causing cancers and other diseases.

• What about the two-sun idea? Our Sun orbits with a twin which we have not yet discovered. It is nicknamed Nemesis. Many stars have twins like this and are called binary stars. When Nemesis comes near us, about every 26 million years, its immense gravity pulls the asteroids orbiting between Mars and Jupiter. They scatter across the solar system, hitting planets as giant meteorites.

EPIDEMICS OF DISEASE?

Maybe the dinosaurs suffered from new diseases, pests or parasites. But it is difficult to imagine one type of germ or pest affecting all the many different kinds of dinosaurs. Also germs or parasites rarely kill off all of their animal victims. Usually some victims become resistant and slowly recover.

Dravidosaurus

RUNNING OUT OF EVOLUTION?

A more biological idea is "evolutionary old age". Just as an individual animal becomes old and weak and finally dies, so does an animal group. The group can no longer evolve to cope with a changing world. It has used up all its genes and is "worn out". The dinosaurs ruled the Earth for about 185 million years. Had they finally become too specialized to adapt? This idea is unlikely, since dinosaurs were still evolving into new types until the very end.

CHANGING PLANTS?

About half-way through the Cretaceous Period, the first flowers appeared on Earth. Perhaps dinosaurs could not digest these new and fast-evolving plants as they quickly took over the landscape. Or maybe the flowering plants made new types of chemicals to defend themselves and the dinosaurs could not survive these poisons.

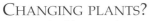

Did early mammals bring about the end of the dinosaurs by eating all their eggs ...

... or were the plant eaters all poisoned as a result of eating the flowering plants that were spreading across the Earth?

THE MASS EGG-STINCTION?

Several mass extinction ideas involve dinosaur eggs. Perhaps new types of small mammals consumed more and more dinosaur eggs. Or dinosaur mothers, weakened by climate change and illness, laid eggs with shells that were too thin. These broke before the babies were ready to hatch and survive.

Did Any Living Things Survive?

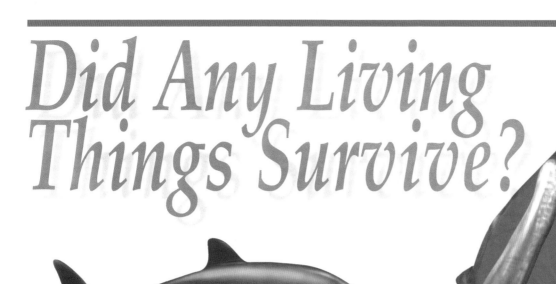

Ichthyosaurs: died out

Birds and mammals, crocodiles, which are close reptile cousins of the dinosaurs, and other types of reptiles, such as turtles, lizards, and snakes, all survived the great extinction on land. In lakes and oceans, many kinds of fish and shellfish also survived and made it into the Tertiary Period.

WHO DIED?

The mass extinction is often called the "Death of the Dinosaurs." It is true that every kind of dinosaur was wiped out. But many other animals disappeared, too:
• The flapping, soaring pterosaurs all perished.
• Large marine reptiles, such as ichthyosaurs, plesiosaurs, and mosasaurs were all gone by the end of the Cretaceous Period. For some the end was sudden. Others had faded millions of years earlier.

Dinosaurs: died out

• Many kinds of fish died out, especially various sharks.
• The shelled marine animals called ammonites and belemnites did not survive. These large animals were mollusks, relatives of today's squid and octopus.
• Not just animals but many kinds of plants died out too.
Overall, some two-thirds to three-quarters of all living things perished, at or near the end of the Cretaceous Period.

WHO SURVIVED?

• Mammals—otherwise, we, as humans, might not be here! The first mammals appeared on Earth at about the same time as the first dinosaurs. They were about the size of mice or rats. As far as we know from fossils, during the entire Age of Dinosaurs no mammal was bigger than a pet cat.

• Some birds. But others which had been around for millions of years suddenly disappeared.

• Crocodiles, turtles, sharks and bony fish.

• Amphibians, such as frogs and newts.

• Insects, spiders, snails, and similar small land creatures.

• Water-dwelling creatures, such as whelks and other marine snails, crabs, shrimps, and other crustaceans, and starfish and other echinoderms.

Birds: some survived

PROBLEMS WITH THEORIES

A reason for the end-of-Cretaceous extinction must explain which life-forms died and which survived. This is a major problem. In particular, why did dinosaurs become extinct while their close cousins the crocodiles did not? The meteorite theory is the most popular, but it still leaves many questions unanswered.

Pterosaurs: died out

COULD DINOSAURS STILL SURVIVE?

There are many legends about great beasts and monsters in remote places, which might be dinosaurs that survived the great extinction:

• Loch Ness, a deep lake in Scotland, could be home to the "Loch Ness monster." Monster hunters describe a creature similar to the plesiosaurs, which lived during the Age of Dinosaurs (see page 196).

• The dense rainforests of the Congo region in Africa may hide beasts that look like sauropod dinosaurs, such as *Diplodocus*.

• The vast Amazon swamps may be home to a fierce *Tyrannosaurus*-like monster that ambushes unwary travelers.

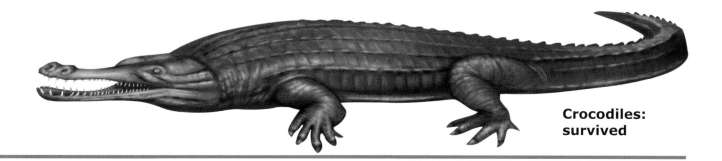

Crocodiles: survived

How Fossils are Formed

1. When a dinosaur died, its remains could become fossilized if they weren't eaten or disturbed.

We know about dinosaurs mainly from their fossils. Most fossils are of hard and tough body parts, such as teeth, bones, claws and horns.

FROM DINOSAUR TO FOSSIL
• A dinosaur died. Its body was washed by a flood on to a river bank. Its flesh, guts and other soft parts were soon eaten by scavengers or rotted away, leaving the bones.
• The river flooded again and covered the bones in mud, sand, silt and other sediments.
• This happened many times as more sediments buried the bones deeper.
• Minerals from the sediments in the water seeped into the bones. Bit by bit they replaced the bone, turning it to solid stone. This took thousands or millions of years.
• The sediments were also squashed by the weight above. The minerals among the sediment particles cemented them into solid rock.

• Over millions of years great earth movements tilted and twisted the layers of sedimentary rocks. Also hot sun, wind, rain, frost, ice, snow and other forces of nature gradually wore away or eroded the upper layers.
• The fossils were uncovered at the surface. One day a fossil expert walks past, looks down and makes another great discovery!

2. As the creature is buried under sediments, the skin and flesh rot away, leaving only the bones.

MOULDS, CASTS AND MUMMIES
Sometimes rock formed around a body part but the part itself was dissolved away to leave an empty place with the same shape. This is a mould fossil.

In other cases, water full of dissolved minerals seeped into the space of a mould fossil. The minerals solidified and gradually filled the gap, forming a cast fossil.

Rarely, a dinosaur perished in a very dry place, such as a desert cave. Its body dried out rapidly without having time to rot. This fast-drying process, mummification, can preserve softer body parts, such as skin. The famous *Tyrannosaurus* fossil "Sue" (see pages 162–3) was preserved like this.

OTHER FOSSILS

Not only dinosaurs left fossils. Other animals did, too, especially those with very hard body parts, such as shells. And especially those which lived in places such as the sea where sediments were plentiful and fossilization was more likely. Plants left fossils, too, especially of their hard bark, cones and seeds. These other fossils show us the animals and plants that lived alongside the dinosaurs.

THE FOSSIL RECORD

Fossils trace the evolution of dinosaurs and other life on Earth. But the fossils we have discovered are only a tiny fraction of the fossils which must exist in rocks all over the world.

TRACE FOSSILS

A true fossil is the remains of an actual body part. A trace fossil did not come from the body itself, but reveals its activity or presence. Trace fossils can be:

- Fossilized footprints or trackways.
- Fossilized tail drags where the tail scraped the ground.
- Fossilized eggshells.
- Fossilized nests made for breeding or sleeping.
- Fossilized signs of gnawing teeth or scratching claws.
- Fossilized droppings. Like bones, these are turned to stone, so they are not soft and smelly! They are known as coprolites and often contain bits and pieces of the last meal.

And these fossils are from only a tiny fraction of all the animals and plants that ever lived. So the fossil record is very selective and patchy – a game of chance.

3. As the bones are buried deeper and deeper, they are changed into rock. They become locked into position by the force of the rocks and sediments above.

4. If the rocks above become worn away by erosion, the fossilized dinosaur bones may become exposed at the surface.

Dinosaur Fossil Hunters

Fossils of dinosaurs can tell us nothing if they are stuck in the ground. Fossil hunters spend years searching remote, dangerous places for fragments of bones and teeth. Their finds have given us our knowledge of dinosaurs.

Barnum Brown outside his tent during one of the digs he led in Alberta, Canada.

MANTELL AND BUCKLAND

In about 1822 English physician Gideon Mantell's wife, discovered some large fossil teeth at a gravel roadworks site in Sussex, England. Mantell was a keen amateur geologist and identified them as reptilian. He showed them to important scientists including William Buckland, Reader of Geology at Oxford University. In 1824 Buckland described a fossil jawbone with long teeth as those of a large, meat-eating reptile which he called *Megalosaurus*. Meanwhile Mantell had discovered the fossil teeth found by his wife were similar to, but bigger than, the teeth of the living iguana lizard. So he named their owner *Iguanodon*, "iguana-tooth".

DINOSAURS COME ALIVE

Another scientist, Richard Owen, examined these various fossils and saw that they were reptiles, but not like any living reptiles such as lizards or crocodiles. In 1841 he described his findings to a British Association for the Advancement of Science meeting in Plymouth, England. He proposed a new name for this group of huge reptiles – Dinosauria. This is when the term "dinosaur" was invented.

THE FIGHT IS ON

Dinosaurs soon gripped people's imaginations. The hunt was on for the biggest and best fossils.

During the late nineteenth century in North America, two teams led by Edward Drinker Cope and Othniel Charles Marsh raced to find the most dinosaurs. They were bitter rivals, but their finds include some of the best known of all dinosaurs such as *Diplodocus* and *Stegosaurus*.

FROM ALBERTA TO THE GOBI DESERT

Barnum Brown of the American Museum of Natural History, explored the Red Deer River of Alberta, Canada from about 1910 –1917. He and his team uncovered fossils of many duck-billed dinosaurs, or hadrosaurs from the Late Cretaceous Period. Henry Fairfield Osborn, director of American Museum of Natural History, described and named *Ornitholestes* in 1903 and *Tyrannosaurus* in 1905. In the 1920s he helped to lead the famous fossil expedition to Mongolia's Gobi Desert when the first fossil dinosaur eggs were found, of *Protoceratops*.

NEW IDEAS

In 1964 American fossil expert, John Ostrom, found the remains of *Deinonychus*. In his report of 1969 he broke with tradition by suggesting it was an active, agile predator with a large brain and complicated behaviour. It was possibly even warm-blooded. Ostrom also suggested that birds evolved from small theropods. From the 1970s Robert Bakker continued to champion the idea that many dinosaurs were warm-blooded. He showed the idea of enormous sauropods, such as *Brachiosaurus* living in water was wrong. Also in the 1970s James Jensen dug up possibly the biggest of all dinosaurs, *Supersaurus* and *Ultrasaurus*. These brachiosaur types were possibly over 30 metres (98 feet) long and weighed over 100 tonnes (98 tons).

DOWN TO SOUTH AMERICA

In 1988 Dr Paul Sereno visited Argentina and found fossils of the very early dinosaur *Herrerasaurus*, a three-metre-long theropod. In 1993 he described the smaller but also very early dinosaur *Eoraptor*. In the late 1990s he explored North Africa and discovered fossils of the 8-metre- (26-foot-) long meat eater *Afrovenator* and the over 20-metre- (66-foot-) sauropod *Jobaria*.

James Jensen poses next to the shoulder blade of *Supersaurus*, one of the huge dinosaurs he uncovered.

Digging up Dinosaurs

Fossil hunters have a lot to do before their very own fossil dinosaur, named after them, can be proudly displayed for the world's news media.

THE RIGHT ROCKS

The first thing that fossil hunters look for is the correct age and type of rock. Dinosaurs lived during the Mesozoic Era, about 250–65 million years ago. Their fossils are found in sedimentary rocks, such as limestones and sandstones. Large-scale geological maps show where Mesozoic sedimentary rocks are found at the Earth's surface rather than buried far below.

FINDING A SITE

Most fossil-bearing rock is part of the top rock layer but this is often hidden under lakes, seas, forests, grassland, and also roads, houses and buildings. Expert fossil hunters frequently need to let nature do the work – they search places where bare surface rocks are continually cracked and worn away by hot sun, strong winds, rain, frost and ice. With luck, the fossils will just be lying there waiting to be picked up! Unfortunately these harsh, rocky places are remote "Badlands", deserts, cliffs, ravines and coasts. There are few roads or towns, so transport is usually a big problem. They are dangerous, too.

MAN-MADE SITES

Fossil hunters also search in places where the actions of people have exposed suitable rocks, such as mines, quarries, rail and road cuttings and deep-foundation building sites. You can do this, too, but you should always get permission and always put safety first.

THE SURVEY

Next, the site must be surveyed. This involves describing the main features, making maps, taking photographs and drawing sketches. A photograph can show a lifelike bird's-eye view. But an illustration can highlight details which may not be obvious in the photograph. The site is usually marked out with pegs and string, like graph paper, so that finds can be located on a grid. These tasks are repeated at intervals as the dig continues.

A team of palaeontologists carefully uncover the fossilized remains of a dinosaur.

DIG, DIG, DIG

At last, the digging can start in earnest. Depending on the size of the specimens, the rock's hardness and other features, fossil hunters use a variety of tools for this:

• Dynamite! Some sites are blown up to expose new rock, and the remains carted away by bulldozers and road diggers.

• Road-drills and jackhammers remove bulk material.

• Picks and shovels clear the area with greater control.

• Small power drills, grinders and sanders move material more carefully.

• Hand-held geological picks, hammers and chisels are used to deal with the more detailed stages.

• Fine needle-probes and even wooden or plastic toothpicks are used for small, delicate items.

    • Brushes are used to clear away very light, crumbly rock.

      • Sieves and shakers sift general debris for small bone fragments or tiny teeth.

ALL WRAPPED UP

Often a fossil is left in its surrounding rock, the matrix. The whole chunk is cut out and taken back to the laboratory, where there is more time and equipment. A delicate fossil can be protected and strengthened by painting it with a resin that soon hardens, or covering it with resin-soaked layers of glass-fibre, or sacking and plaster of Paris, or by using spray-on foam that quickly dries and hardens. A wooden or metal cradle built around the whole block allows it to be lifted from a wheelbarrow to a heavy-lift cargo helicopter.

Dinosaurs in Museums

A jumbled pile of fossil bones fresh from the dig site is only the start of putting a dinosaur together. There may be years of careful cleaning, measuring, comparing, copying and rebuilding, before the skeleton or a lifelike model is put on display in a top museum.

A GOOD CLEAN-UP

First the fossils must be cleaned of their surrounding rock. This is very time-consuming. Often it is done under the microscope with small sanders, vibrating needles and high-speed dentist's drills. Shot-blasting fires a powerful stream of sand or plastic grains at the area. If the surrounding rock is different from the fossil rock, acids and other chemicals can be used to dissolve it away in stages, leaving the fossil unharmed. This can take months in acid baths.

FILLING IN THE GAPS

A complete fossil skeleton of a dinosaur is a rare find. Usually the remains are bent and broken, jumbled and mixed up, with various parts missing. The gaps are "filled in" using parts from another, similar dinosaur, or from similar animals that we know from today, such as crocodiles, lizards and birds. This is the science of comparative anatomy. (Anatomy studies the structures and parts of living things.)

MAKING COPIES

A complete fossil skeleton is very heavy and awkward to handle, since it is made of solid rock. One brachiosaur toe bone is far too heavy to lift! Also a very rare specimen may be worth more than its weight in gold! So copies of the fossils are made in glass-fiber or similar material, and painted to look like the originals. Then the originals can be stored safely.

A museum worker cleans up pieces of a dinosaur fossil discovered during a dig.

MOUNTING THE SKELETON

Finally the skeleton is mounted – put together with bones linked as they would have been in life. Older mounted skeletons had thick metal bars or wires to hold them up. Today a lightweight metal or plastic frame is used. This is almost invisible since it follow the curves of the body and the insides of the glass-fibre "bones". Modern museum displays also put dinosaurs in exciting positions and surroundings that tell us more about their life. They may be fighting off a predator, looking after their babies or roaring at the visitors.

MAKING A LIFELIKE MODEL

Comparative anatomy is also used to add muscles, guts and other soft parts of a dinosaur to its skeleton. Living bones have roughened areas where muscles are anchored. These rough patches or scars may show on fossils, revealing the sizes and positions of a dinosaur's muscles. The position and size of the lungs and heart can be guessed at from the structure of the rib cage. The stomach and intestines are added in, again using modern reptiles and other animals as guides.

CLOTHED IN SKIN

Gradually the dinosaur is rebuilt from its skeleton outwards, layer by layer. On the outside is skin. Rare fossils of dinosaur skin show that they had scales like modern reptiles. Some had bony plates and spines too, although the positioning of these is often the result of clever guesswork.

WHAT COLOUR?

The final touch is colour. But this, we do not know. Fossil skin is made of stone and is the colour of stone. So you can colour a dinosaur any way you wish, even pink with yellow spots, and no one could say it was wrong! However, most dinosaur models have colours and patterns based on similar animals today, such as crocodiles and lizards.

Using lifting platforms, specialist dinosaur builders assemble the pieces of a model *Barosaurus* skeleton.

Timeline

Xiaosaurus

Janenschia

125

Bar

150

175

200

Coelophysis

Yangchuanosaurus

Seismo

Mamenchisaurus

Lesothosaurus

Brachiosaurus

Diplo

Zigongo

Plateosaurus

Apatos

Kentrosaurus

Riojasaurus

Megalosaurus

Stegosaurus

Triassic

Jurassic

This timeline shows when the dinosaurs
that are featured in this book were alive.
They are not shown to scale.

Wannanasaurus

Ornithomimus

100   75   50   **Millions of years ago**

Gallimimus

Euoplocephalus

Parasaurolophus

sognathus

Gigantosaurus

Edmontosaurus

Protoceratops

s

Maiasaura

Spinosaurus

Hypsilophodon

Triceratops

Ankylosaurus

s

Notoceratops

Albertosaurus

Psittacosaurus

Deinonychus

Tyrannosaurus

Oviraptor

Styracosaurus

asaurus   Iguanodon

Corythosaurus

Velociraptor

urus

Minmi

Stegoceras

Pachycephalosaurus

Tröodon

Cretaceous

Quaternary

Index

England 6, 7
Eoraptor 21, 71
Eoraptor lunensis 21
epidemics 64
Equator 61
Erythrosuchus 20
Euoplocephalus 34
Europe 10, 61
evolution 65
extinctions 17, 58—67
eyesight 40—41

F
feathers 52—3
feet 46—7
ferns 13
fighting 32—3
food chain 28
footprints 46—7
fossil formation 68—9
fossil hunters 70—71, 72—3
France 9, 25

G
Germany 25
Gerrothorax 18
global warming 61
greenhouse gases 61
Greenland 61

H
hadrosaurs 31, 34, 44, 70
Herrerasaurus 71
hunting techniques 33
Hylonomus 18
Hypacrosaurus 31
Hyperodapedon 18

I
ichthyosaurs 13, 19, 66
Iguanadon 24, 51, 70
India 61
intelligence 38—9
iridium 62, 63

J
Jensen, J. 71
Jobaria 71
Jupiter 64
Jurassic Period 9, 10, 12—13, 25
   meat-eaters 26

plant-eaters 29, 30
K
K-T boundary 58
Kannameyeria 19
Kentrosaurus 39
Komodo dragon 54—5

L
Leaellynasaura 45
life 14—15
Loch Ness monster 67

M
magma 11
Mantell, G. 70
Mars 64
Marsh, O. 70
mass extinctions 58—9, 66
meat-eating dinosaurs 24—7
Megalosaurus 70
Mesozoic Era 9, 11, 28, 58, 72
meteorites 61, 62, 63, 64, 67
Mexico 63
Miller, S. 15
models 75
Mongolia 26, 30, 70
mosasaurs 66
moulds 68—9
mummies 68—9
museums 74—5

N
Nemesis 64
nests 44—5
neutrinos 65
North Africa 71
North America 25, 27, 29, 30, 32
   fossils 59
   riverbanks 37
   volcanoes 61

O
Ododromeus 45
Ordovician Period 16
organic molecules 15
ornithischia 22, 23
Ornitholestes 70
Ornithomimus 27
ornithopods 23
Osnorn, H.F. 70
Owen, R. 70